Secrets of Top-Performing Salespeople

THE ALLIGATOR TRAP

How to Sell without Being Turned into a Pair of Shoes

EDWARD R. DEL GAIZO

KEVIN J. CORCORAN

DAVID J. ERDMAN

IRWIN
Professional Publishing©
Chicago • London • Singapore

This publication is designed to provide accurate and
authoritative information in regard to the subject matter
covered. It is sold with the understanding that neither the
author or the publisher is engaged in rendering legal, accounting,
or other professional service. If legal advice or other expert
assistance is required, the services of a competent professional
person should be sought.

From a Declaration of Principles jointly adopted by a Committee
of the American Bar Association and a Committee of Publishers.

Times Mirror
Higher Education Group

Library of Congress Cataloging-in-Publication Data

Del Gaizo, Edward R.
  The alligator trap : how to sell without being turned into a pair
of shoes/Edward R. Del Gaizo, Keven J. Corcoran, David J. Erdman.
    p. cm.
  Includes index
  ISBN: 0-7863-0856-7
  1. Selling. 2. Sales management. I. Corcoran, Kevin J., 1954-
II. Erdman, David J. III. Title
  HF5438.25 D45 96
  658.85'20—dc20   96-19416

Printed in the United States of America
1 2 3 4 5 6 7 8 9 0 BP 3 2 1 0 9 8 7 6

We dedicate this book to the salespeople of the world, who work tirelessly for the benefit of their customers, who are a key source of innovation and progress in organizations, who deliver every day and wear the title salesperson *with commitment and integrity. You bring great honor to our profession.*

PREFACE

Through four decades of research, Learning International has conducted numerous studies on successful organizations and their salespeople. From this research, the authors of this book have pulled together 19 important lessons inspired by top salespeople, their managers, and their customers. These lessons, grouped into four sections, are compact, digestible, and practical. Quotes and anecdotes from interviews that the authors conducted with salespeople and customers serve to illustrate key points.

No matter what you sell—from poultry to financial services, from telecommunications to turbine engines—the following pages will be relevant to you. These lessons aren't tricks or "guerrilla" gimmicks. They're well-researched practices and tips that will contribute to your ability to build a solid base of strong, profitable relationships.

Share these tips with your friends and colleagues in sales. Help them to avoid the *alligator trap,* a condition that too many salespeople have created for themselves.

Daniel B. Baitch, Ph.D.
Co-author, *High Performance Sales Organizations:
Creating Competitive Advantage in the Global Market*

ACKNOWLEDGMENTS

There are many individuals who have had a part in the making of this book. Certainly the many salespeople, their sales managers, and customers whom we have interviewed or studied over the past several decades deserve the foremost mention. Without them, this book would not have been possible. Some of the stories and quotes we collected since formally beginning this book belong to the following individuals and their organizations: Mike Bailey, Jostens Printing and Publishing Division; Kay Bruner, Henry Ford Health Systems; Brandt Burghoff, American Savings Bank; Jim Crossley, Sterling Software; Lisa Fawcett, Fisons Corporation; Lt. Col. Bob Foley, United States Marine Corps; Dave Good, Sterling Software; Steve Herbert, American Savings Bank; Ray Lawlor, American Savings Bank; Patty Racovitz, American Savings Bank; Toni Rose, BTI Office Products International; Victoria Reback, American Savings Bank; Jim Shultenover, Marriott Hotels; and Bill White, Great Financial Bank.

The following colleagues provided valuable insights—guiding us into the right direction—by either reviewing early drafts of the book or simply contributing their wisdom: Leslie Aitken, Ed Becker, Carol Burke, Renee Cabanelas, Joe Corcoran, Bob Cronin, Kathy David, Debra Dinnocenzo, Sandi Edwards, Mike Frank, Jo Gallico, Andrea Glanz, John Hine, Howard Kamens, Lynn Kimmel, Mark Little, Jennifer Long, Steve Lunz, Linda Osborne, MaryAnn Masarech, Jim Ninivaggi, Ed Odachowski, Carlos Quintero, Mike Radick, John Rainforth, Zena Robles, Betts Silver, Stacy Sullivan, Polly Thompson, and Joe Trueblood.

It is hard to single out a few individuals, but the following contributed their time and effort to ensure that this book ended up in your hands rather than sank into the depths of the quagmire: Dan Baitch, Lucy Curran, Helen Frith, Judy Hanley, Valery Shields Moore, and Clem Russo.

CONTENTS

ONE

ESTABLISHING
THE CUSTOMER
RELATIONSHIP

At first he looked like a regular guy. But soon, after the small talk ebbed, you noticed a gradual but dramatic change in his appearance. His eyes began to shrink, and you began to wonder whether he could even see the problem you were trying to solve. His ears all but disappeared and you began to doubt whether he could hear your needs—or whether he even cared to listen. His mouth grew larger and his teeth chattered a cacophony of irrelevant facts and data—specifications and trivia about his offering that you didn't care to know. He asked few questions and those that he did ask showed he hadn't taken the time to do his homework. This and his cold-blooded, drooling gaze led you to believe that he didn't quite have your best interest at heart.

When you stated an objection or concern, he got more agitated. Far from feeling like a "valued customer," you began to feel more like "the consumed." You were prey. You were revenue in a duck pond. You had fallen into the jaws of an alligator.

Your thoughts turned away from whatever concern or problem you hoped to solve. You scanned the environment for an escape route. Eventually you were freed from captivity.

The salesperson did not succeed. He was a victim who created his own snare—he fell into the alligator trap.

If you work in sales, you probably pay close attention to the actions of the salespeople who try to sell to you. And if you're like most people, you have already encountered the salesperson in the story you've just read. He, and others like him, suffer from a common misconception about what it means to be a salesperson. In its continuing effort to understand the art of selling, Learning International's Research Team interviewed customers of some of the most successful salespeople in the country. When asked what distinguishes top salespeople from the rest, one customer said:

> Top salespeople are much better listeners. By listening, they're able to understand my situation and earn my trust. But most people are like alligators. They've got little eyes, little ears, and great big mouths.

Since then, we have used the term *alligator trap* to describe salespeople who transform themselves into destructive creatures who make potential customers feel more like prey than partners. Many customers have felt the frustration of "alligator wrestling"—trying to work with distasteful salespeople who blemish the profession. How do you ensure that you won't morph into this dreaded reptilian rogue? By using some of the many approaches we'll explore in the next several chapters.

Perhaps the most important thing you can do to combat your alligator tendencies is to establish strong customer relationships. Creating long-term customer relationships is critical to sales organizations. Why? Because in this age of increased competition, it helps to have loyal and satisfied customers. Customers are an important source of recommendations and referrals. They tend to generate repeat sales. And as the cost of starting up new business relationships continues to rise, partnerships with existing customers are usually more profitable for sales organizations.

How do you create long-term relationships? Corporations today are leaner and meaner. Many don't have time for the schmooze mentality of the '80s. Instead, clients are really looking for those who will help them attain competitive advantage and stay on top in the global marketplace.

> The purpose of the salesperson today is to build the business and influence customer loyalty.

One of our clients is a perfect example of how important the concept of competitive advantage has become in sales. This company, a major designer and fabricator of trade show exhibits, found that many of its customers were putting routine decisions about trade shows on the back burner and focusing more on global issues and concerns. To renew interest in its product, the company developed a new sales approach: to demonstrate to its customers the *strategic* value of trade shows and then provide the marketing services and sales support that would make the trade show experience more profitable for them. Though this approach proved highly successful, it depended strongly on one key element: salespeople who could act as consultants with customers and work closely with them to achieve differentiation from their competitors.

As this example shows, today's salespeople must work hard to create value for the long term, developing customized solutions that enhance the profits of their customers' companies and their own organization. They must demonstrate an in-depth knowledge of their customers' needs—and understand how those needs may change over time. And they must recognize the greater pressures customers work under today and the new roles customers play as strategic decision makers.

It's necessary to establish a trust-oriented relationship between the salesperson and the customer, one that goes beyond simply buying and selling. And the salesperson's personality and skills are the key to success here.

How can they do all this? In the following pages, we'll give you several valuable techniques. They'll demonstrate what you need to do to establish your integrity and credibility with customers and meet what our research in the United States, Europe, and Japan has shown are the highest expectations customers today have about the salesperson:

- A salesperson who keeps promises.
- A salesperson who knows his or her product or service.
- A salesperson who is honest.

Once the customer relationship is established, the salesperson can focus on other important elements of the sales process, such as coordinating the efforts of several different functions within their own organization and leading a sales team. Or communicating with various departments at a company to facilitate the delivery of products and services. The point is: Salespeople today need to be good at more than just making the sale. Without a strong customer relationship as the foundation, the other tactics you use to get and keep business become irrelevant.

DO YOUR HOMEWORK

—Be Prepared

Alligator Trap
Attacking in the Dark

"Sometimes you win; sometimes you lose; sometimes you get rained out. But you always have to get dressed for the game."

The first trap alligators fall into is failing to prepare for their encounters. When they see prospective prey, they don't think about their approach, they simply lunge. For good salespeople, however, planning is one of the cornerstones to success. If you don't have goals for your business and professional development, you'll go nowhere. That's why all successful salespeople must continually pursue new areas of knowledge, review and upgrade their prospecting capabilities, and develop more effective presentation skills. New salespeople experience a particularly steep learning curve because they have a lot to digest all at once: process, product, customers, organizational structures, and policy.

Preparation and practice are critical to sales success. The best salespeople not only know *what* skills and knowledge to apply during a sale, they also determine *how* to apply them for maximum impact. They also work continuously to perfect their sales approach and improve their sales performance.

DEVELOP THE PROPER SALES MIND-SET

To be a success in sales today, the first step is to start thinking of yourself not just as a salesperson, but as a business expert.

To provide the right products and services to customers—and come up with appropriate solutions to customer problems—it's not enough to be well versed in the features and benefits of what you sell. You also have to know about your customers' needs, the environment of the marketplace, and the many factors influencing business today. And you have to know how to position what you sell to show your customers how you can truly satisfy their needs.

Above all, you must serve as a true business *resource* for customers. This means:

■ *Educating and informing customers.* Customers today are more educated and knowledgeable than ever before, but they still look to you for new information about the business world, emerging markets, and new competitors. You can increase your business knowledge in several ways, which we'll discuss shortly.

■ *Solving customer problems.* Customers today have more responsibility than before and work under greater bottom-line pressures. They seek your help in coming up with cost-effective solutions to their business problems. By establishing your credibility and trustworthiness with customers, you encourage them to confide in you about their problems.

■ *Advising customers on how to gain competitive advantage.* Customers today face more intense and more global competition. They expect you to help them figure out new ways to stay ahead of their competitors. A good way to do this is to come up with solutions that help customers improve their image, their productivity, or the quality of their product or service.

One airline we've worked with, for example, has consistently received high ratings in service and performance by encouraging its salespeople to respond quickly and flexibly to the ever-changing needs of its corporate and travel agent accounts. By applying a consultative approach to solving customer problems and by demonstrating superior product knowledge—whether in the travel agency arena, in cargo sales, or with meetings and conventions programs—the salespeople for this airline have helped their company rank either number one or number two in the biggest markets nationwide.

> There is an evolution from product selling, where you are selling features and benefits of a product and driving a product into a specific market, to a shift toward satisfying the customer's total requirements.

INCREASE YOUR BODY OF KNOWLEDGE

Knowledge is key to improving your opportunity in every prospective account. So seek the information you need to make a positive impression on your prospects and to meet their business needs, and set goals for each of your accounts. What information do you need to achieve your goals? Four areas of knowledge are especially critical:

- *General business knowledge.* Today's customers want to talk with salespeople who are well read, understand the marketplace, and follow market trends. So keep abreast of business news and market conditions by doing your homework daily: Read annual reports, trade publications, and product information; maintain memberships in professional or business organizations; and watch cable news programs that focus on timely business issues.

- *Product knowledge.* Today's customers don't have time to become experts in what you're selling. They rely on your expertise to demonstrate how your product or service can meet their needs. So make sure you know your products and services cold: specs, features and benefits, business issues they address, delivery schedules, and service details.

- *Company and industry knowledge.* Customers are relying on fewer suppliers these days, so they put a high value on salespeople who know them and their industry intimately. They don't have time to educate you about their organization. They want to be reassured from the start that you know what *they* do, what customers *they* sell to, who *their* competitors are, and how your product or service can support *their* corporate strategies.

> In the future, salespeople will become brokers of knowledge. Direct knowledge or access to knowledge will be critical to sales success.

- *Knowledge of your competition.* To evaluate just how much time and effort you should invest in a prospective customer, use your business contacts to find out who your competition is. What's the nature of their relationship with the prospect? How long have they been working together? How satisfied is the prospect in dealing with your competition? What are the advantages of the products and services your competitor offers? How do you compare in terms of what you can offer? How can you gain a competitive edge?

PROSPECT FOR CUSTOMERS

The sales process begins with prospecting. Some leads, but not all, will become qualified prospects. Good prospects can be identified and approached: They have a clear need or want, have the ability to pay, and have the authority to buy.

While an alligator—driven by hunger—might go after a prospect without preparation, a good salesperson knows better. Before you approach a prospect, be sure you know in advance who the appropriate contact person is and what strategy you will employ when you meet that person. And don't approach your contact until you've researched the company's products and services, customers, and competitors. That knowledge will help you to ask truly *relevant* questions, which enhances your ability to help the customer.

Another valuable tip when prospecting: Avoid making cold calls. They are often perceived as interruptions to the workday, and they can irritate the customer. Cold calls can also be frustrating for you. No matter how much time you prepare for the call, you rarely achieve good results when you approach a prospect unannounced. In almost every case,

> Know who are prospects and who are suspects. Use your research skills and talk to the pros in your industry to identify top producers and the buying centers within an organization. Manage the relationship from the very beginning.

customers are more receptive to you when you schedule a meeting beforehand.

PREPARE FOR THE SALES CALL

You should develop a strategy and a follow-up plan for each prospecting call. A good plan saves time for the prospect and you. The most productive sales calls are those in which you use a structured approach to gather critical information, uncover customer needs, and identify ways to help the customer.

Make sure that each of your prospecting calls has specific, realistic, and measurable objectives. Perhaps you want the prospect to become familiar with one or two of your products by attending demonstrations. Or maybe you're seeking a simple commitment from the prospect to call several of your established customers. Whatever your goals, you won't know whether you've achieved them if you can't observe or measure them.

After you've done your homework on the prospect, ask yourself the following questions:

- What business knowledge do you have that might be of interest to this prospect?
- What business or industry trends might directly affect this prospect?
- What are the key business strategies and goals in the prospect's organization?
- What do you want to say about the prospect's products or services?
- What do you want to say that will differentiate you from your competition?

Next, you should try to become acquainted with the different buying centers and decision makers within the prospect's organization. Ask yourself:

- Do I have something of value that will benefit any of these buying groups?
- Which buying group will benefit the most from what I have to offer?
- Which buying group is most likely to make a purchase at this time?
- Which buying group has the most influence within the organization?

In addition, set an agenda with your customer for each call. The most productive sales calls are those that have a defined objective. So, to avoid wasting resources and time—both yours and your customer's—establish what you plan to discuss with the customer each time you meet. (If the customer doesn't agree with your agenda, allow him or her to propose one.) Then, at the end of each call, evaluate what's been accomplished and what still needs to be done. Recap the agreed-upon activities (and the people responsible for those actions).

> **Top salespeople aim accurately so they don't waste any time. They aim at specific targets.**

Show the customer how productive and efficient you are by helping him or her understand what you can accomplish with each meeting.

The best salespeople have an ability to organize themselves and their customers. They spend a lot of time planning what they need to do to achieve goals so they don't waste time. Being well prepared for each sales call allows you to:

- *Respond better to customer questions or objections.* If you have a good understanding of your prospect, the products and services the prospect sells, and the prospect's current business issues, it's much less likely that you'll be surprised by questions or objections you didn't anticipate.

- *Minimize the risk of failing to achieve your objectives.* Careful preparation helps you to keep your conversation on track, promotes a more productive discussion, and improves your chances of meeting your call objectives.
- *Maintain your self-confidence.* By doing your homework beforehand, you're in a much better position to establish your authority and expertise, and that's bound to boost your self-confidence.

GAIN SUPPORT FROM YOUR OWN ORGANIZATION

Support from your own organization is critical to your success in preparing for and making sales calls. A defined sales process and state-of-the-art technology should be in place. Your entire organization should be committed to a strong customer focus, and be ready to support and deliver on your solution to the customer's needs.

> The organization needs to support its salespeople by introducing a good information system and by giving good technical and software support.

High-performing sales organizations have well-defined sales processes. A defined process, managed from beginning to end, makes you more efficient and more effective. To determine if you're getting the kind of support you need from your organization, ask these questions:

- What are your organization's best steps for dealing with customers—from prospecting through follow-up after implementation?
- Is there a system in place for getting proposals carried out?

- Has your organization identified specific best practices to use for prospecting?
- What are the other components of your sales process?

Successful sales organizations also have an excellent database of prospects and customers. They equip their salespeople with up-to-date technology—both hardware and software—that provides information at their fingertips. Top salespeople utilize contact management software that stores and tracks information on each customer, have product knowledge information (and even training) right on their laptops, and use their portable computers to their maximum advantage.

To do your job efficiently and effectively, make sure your company equips you with the right processes, tools, and technologies.

> **One-on-one contact has always been an important element in sales, and it will continue to be so in the future.**

More Tips

- *Insist on making in-person sales calls.* Meeting with prospects face-to-face is still the most effective way to learn about them, to determine how you can meet their needs, and to make a sale. When calling for an appointment, don't let the prospect draw you into giving a sales presentation over the phone. Explain that the purpose of your call is to make a specific appointment, not to make a sale. A good way to get their attention: Begin your phone conversation with a strong business statement that explains how the meeting will be useful to the prospect.

- *Live up to customer expectations.* Today's customers are more knowledgeable and more demanding than ever, and they have higher expectations of the salespeople they do business with. Beginning with the first interaction, customers look for evidence of good business knowledge in salespeople, a strong sense of professionalism, and the ability to ask insightful, "big picture" questions. To live up to customer expectations, prepare extensively for each prospecting call and conduct yourself with confidence and authority.

- *Develop rapport with customers.* It's especially important to establish a comfortable relationship with prospects and new customers right from the start. The best way to do this is to engage in "small talk" before you get down to business. This creates a pressure-free environment and allows the customer get to know you on a personal level. How do you know when to stop making small talk? In most cases, the customer will start to redirect the conversation toward business when he or she is ready to talk shop.

> **If you can't develop rapport, you'll never get the customer to share information.**

- *Maintain the right attitude for selling.* While enthusiasm and positive thinking are critical to successful selling, having the right attitude involves a lot more. It also means being sensitive to the customer's feelings, being flexible to accommodate the customer's needs, and being friendly but businesslike throughout the sales process. The most successful salespeople are characterized by a sense of integrity and professionalism, and they consistently maintain a strong problem-solving approach.

- *Analyze your successes and failures.* Critique your performance after every prospecting call by asking yourself: How did I handle myself? Did I achieve my goal? Then analyze your successes and failures, and evaluate and redirect your efforts as needed. If necessary, ask for help. Having someone more experienced observe and critique you can change your entire career for the better. Don't be afraid to try new methods. If your prospecting efforts aren't working, try another approach.

■ *Be systematic and organized.* Selling is a complicated process that often requires you to stay close to large numbers of customers over long periods of time. To do it well, it's important to be systematic and organized—and that means keeping good records:

> The best salespeople focus clearly on what they have to achieve to be successful. They're constantly measuring themselves against their targets. They're very goal oriented.

1. Create a file for each of your prospects and accounts.
2. Include news articles or industry reports that may pertain to each customer.
3. Document customer reactions during your meetings.
4. Take notes on what's important to the customer.
5. Write down agreed-upon next steps.

2

BUILD PARTNERSHIPS

Alligator Trap
Devour Your Prey in One Sitting

Alligators aren't interested in being partners. They prefer to be predators. They don't want to take the time to build mutually beneficial relationships. But being a good salesperson requires that you ally yourself with anyone you consider a customer. Only by working to create win-win relationships can you ensure repeat business with customers and win their loyalty.

CARE ABOUT YOUR CUSTOMERS

Customers want to do business with salespeople who consistently deliver on their promises and who are willing to go the extra mile. They value the intangible aspects of their relationship with a supplier—dependability, professionalism, accessibility, and creativity—far more than the tangible factors related to a product or service.

Customers want to deal with salespeople who truly *care* about them and about building a long-term relationship. In interviews conducted with the customers of 24 leading sales organizations, we were told that customers value a salesperson who:

> After a sales call, the best salespeople ask themselves, "How did the customer feel about the call?" Other salespeople ask, "How did I feel about the call?"

- Puts the customer's needs first.
- Is well informed about the customer's business and industry.
- Is always courteous, friendly, and easy to do business with.
- Comes through for customers.
- Maintains frequent contact with customers.
- Expresses a desire to help the customer's business grow.
- Doesn't pressure the customer to buy.
- Remains accessible even after a sale.

We heard one story, for example, where a salesperson helped a client beef up an internal presentation she had to give by providing research support, developing attractive overheads, and locating several subject matter experts to be interviewed. Though the presentation was totally unrelated to the salesperson's efforts to promote his product, his assistance to the client contributed significantly to demonstrating his value as a resource and his commitment to building a long-term relationship.

BE HONEST AND TRUSTWORTHY

Trust, based on the salesperson's personal integrity and commitment, is a critical element in a successful business partnership. When customers believe they can trust you, they're much more likely to spend time with you, share important information with you, and continue to buy from you. They're also more likely to recommend you to others in their organization and to friends and colleagues in other companies. If you have a relationship with somebody, for example, you can live through pricing problems and you can live through bad delivery problems, you can live through anything as long as you can trust him or her.

How do you build trust with customers?

- *Be honest.* If you can't answer a question, refer the customer to another source—even if it's a competitor. If what you have to offer doesn't satisfy the customer's needs, say so. Your success is built in large part on your integrity.

- *Be realistic.* Set clear expectations about your product, quality, delivery, and follow-through right from the start. Don't make promises to customers that you can't keep.

- *Be up front.* Don't let a potential problem remain unsolved. Resolve issues openly and respond honestly to customer concerns.

- *Do what's right.* Make recommendations on the basis of your customer's needs, not on what you need to sell. Turn down the business if it's not in the customer's long-term interests.

ESTABLISH YOUR CREDIBILITY

The credibility of the salesperson is also a critical factor in developing long-term business partnerships. When you establish credibility with your customers, you win their respect and confidence and earn the right to participate in their decision making. When you have credibility, customers are more likely to think favorably of your products and services—and of your organization—and they'll take your recommendations more seriously.

How do you establish credibility with customers?

■ *Demonstrate your knowledge.* Being well informed shows customers that you know what you're talking about and that you're the kind of person they should be doing business with.

■ *Highlight your credentials.* Being able to say that you've given speeches at business gatherings, written articles, or participated in panel discussions helps establish you as an expert with your customers.

> Build your credibility by returning calls promptly, by answering messages in a timely manner, and by getting things done for the customer.

■ *Practice good communication skills.* Being able to articulate ideas clearly and communicate effectively creates a positive impression on customers.

■ *Maintain the proper attitude.* Being friendly but businesslike convinces customers that you're a true professional.

■ *Keep commitments.* Being punctual and reliable establishes you as salesperson that customers can always count on.

CREATE VALUE FOR THE CUSTOMER

The best business partner is one who creates value. Thus, top salespeople always try to function as strategic problem solvers for their customers. They share their customer's vision and are continually finding new ways to help their customer be more successful and bringing about more innovative and distinctive solutions that add value for the customer.

Customers place a high value on salespeople who can help them meet their business goals and the needs of their internal and external customers. The salesperson who creates value for the customer in these ways becomes an ally—a trusted advisor and a valuable resource.

How do you become a strategic problem solver for customers?

- *Uncover strategic needs.* Don't focus solely on the customer's *stated* need. Through effective probing, determine the need behind the need—a strategic goal or business objective that the customer wants to achieve.

- *Develop creative solutions.* Address the customer's strategic needs in the most efficient and effective manner possible. Consider a customized version of your product, for example, or a mix of products and services.

> The way of working with a customer needs to be less one of confrontation and more of how can we both gain something? Customers today expect more help and support from their suppliers.

- *Arrive at mutually beneficial agreements.* First, work with the customer to develop a common understanding of the issues at hand. Then try to reach a solution that makes sense for your organization and the customer's.

One salesperson we know of practiced these strategies when working for an information processing systems and software company. One of his clients, a major New England distributor of car parts for large auto body shops, had decided to install a new system to improve inventory control and asked him to present a possible solution. In conducting interviews with managers within the client organization and some of its major customers, the salesperson made an important discovery: Inventory problems were causing significant delays in purchase orders and having an adverse impact on body shop scheduling.

The salesperson recommended a customized solution that linked the distributor to the shops it supplied and allowed customers to research the availability of parts themselves and place orders instantly. While expensive, the new system paid off handsomely in increased business and improved customer satisfaction.

More Tips

- *Maintain a two-way dialogue.* The most productive business partnerships are those that achieve a free and open exchange of information and ideas. So, when conducting sales calls, try not to dominate the conversation or come across as if you're interrogating the customer. A good way to maintain a two-person dialogue is to routinely ask for feedback from the customer whenever you present a new idea or recommend a solution. Top salespeople are skilled at understanding customer needs based on this two-way communication. Salespeople won't succeed if they suggest the ace of clubs when the customer needs the ace of hearts.

- *Go to bat for the customer.* To become partners with your customer, you have to show that you're on the customer's side. That means going to bat for the customer within your own company, working to make the customer look good in the eyes of his or her colleagues and superiors, and providing assistance and information even when there's no prospect of an immediate sale.

- *Build bridges with the customer.* A key step in building a long-term customer relationship is to establish your interest in helping to make the customer succeed. Take the opportunity to demonstrate your interest every time you meet with the customer: Acknowledge and empathize with the customer's concerns, confirm your understanding of the customer's needs, and ask what you can do to make things better for the customer. Sales reps with good empathy skills can get on with a wide variety of customers, and they can develop rapport quickly.

■ *Always keep the customer informed.* One of the best ways to foster customer confidence is to include the customer in all major decisions related to the sale and to keep the customer informed at every step of the sales cycle. Of course, there's no need to overwhelm customers with trivial matters, but if a customer has to call you to find out the status of the sale, you missed the boat.

3

CREATE AND DELIVER COMPELLING PRESENTATIONS

Alligator Trap
Your Mere Presence Impacts Others

Alligators aren't used to preparing themselves before a meeting. They emerge from the swamp and are often not a pretty sight. No wonder others run from them. They don't understand that first impressions can sometimes make or break a deal and whether you're meeting with one person or with a large group, it is critical that you be prepared.

> *"It was my first day on the job for a company that designed local area networks, and I was assigned to make a customized presentation for a $75,000 contract. I had no understanding of the audience. . . nor did I realize that their decision would be made that very day. I wasn't prepared, hadn't done enough homework, and didn't really know what the customer was looking for. To make matters worse, my presentation was slipshod and casual. . .*

Needless to say, I flopped miserably, though I didn't realize it until the group decided to caucus and then announced that they were going with a competitor. I tried to backpedal, ask questions, and then get a hold on their needs, but it was too late."

Many salespeople have had training in preparing and making presentations. But even those that have made many presentations aren't experts. Some seasoned salespeople fail to do their homework or to double-check on logistics and details. Some recruit additional presenters who are not well versed in the customer's needs, priorities, and goals.

> You have to focus on what's important to the customer before you start to talk.

The most successful salespeople exercise critical judgment before they bring someone else into a presentation. They're especially careful not to waste the customer's time. They stick to the allotted time frame. They review their agenda beforehand with the customer, and ask for any changes or additions. And they're flexible enough to make adjustments during the presentation, if necessary. Above all, top salespeople do their homework and know their audience's priorities.

REFLECT CUSTOMER NEEDS

No matter how polished your communication skills, your presentation will lead nowhere unless you demonstrate a clear understanding of your customer's needs.

The best salespeople use an audience-centered approach when making presentations. They make sure to customize their presentation to their audience, and reflect the specific needs of their different audience members.

Remember that your primary objective in making a presentation is to show how you can solve a customer problem or help the customer make improvements in product quality, customer satisfaction, and market share. Use your presentation to explain how you will do that, and provide details to back up what you say. Outline:

- Your understanding of the problem to be solved.
- Your recommendation or solution.
- Your organization's capabilities.
- Your implementation plan.
- Your delivery schedule.
- Your service strategy.
- The financial investment involved.
- The time frame for completion..

Throughout the presentation, try to relate the features and benefits of your product or service to the customer's business issues and strategic goals. Show how you can satisfy the customer's:

- *Financial needs:* How will your solution increase revenues or control costs for the customer?
- *Performance needs:* How will your solution maintain or improve productivity for the customer?
- *Image needs:* How will your solution improve the customer's image or the prestige of the customer's company?

> Customers will always test you to see what you can do for them.

Make sure your presentation is clear, logical, and persuasive. The extent to which you do this indicates how well you understand the customer's needs and how effectively you can guide the customer in achieving his or her objectives.

WATCH YOUR LANGUAGE

It's also important that you use language that's familiar to your audience and that ensures understanding and interest.

- Avoid technical jargon.
- Speak at your audience's level of knowledge and sophistication.
- Don't try to impress your audience with big or fancy words; that will only distract or alienate them.
- Try to avoid cumbersome phrasing such as "inasmuch as" or "at this point in time."
- Reinforce your presentation by using appropriate communication tools, such as samples, stories, testimonials, and demonstrations, as well as visual aids. These improve your audience's understanding of your product or service, and also help you capture and hold your audience's attention.
- Keep graphics simple and relevant.
- When presenting financial or statistical information, try to avoid "data overload." Don't get caught in complex numbers unless you definitely know that you're dealing with an audience that wants to see everything broken out.

Salespeople have to be good at presenting a package once they understand what the customer requires.

Probe during the presentation to uncover how much your audience understands and buys into your ideas. Then probe afterwards to find out how well the presentation went. Ask: Did I meet your expectations? Did I cover the agreed-upon agenda? Did I respond effectively to questions or concerns? One salesperson notes, "I clarify how the product works, but I put the burden on myself for not being clear. I might suggest that we walk through the issues again. That doesn't make the client feel defensive."

PRACTICE...PRACTICE...PRACTICE

To make sure your presentation is as informative and convincing as possible, practice beforehand. Select an environment that will be free from interruptions, and rehearse in front of colleagues, friends, family members, or a mirror. Always time yourself to make sure you don't exceed the time allotted for your presentation.

As you practice, remember these delivery tips:

■ *Maintain eye contact.* The best way to develop rapport with your audience is to look people squarely in the eye. Start by focusing on the most receptive faces, then gradually turn your gaze toward others in the room.

■ *Watch your body language.* Don't stay glued to one spot. If you have the freedom to walk around while you're talking, do so. Avoid meaningless gestures or nervous habits that may distract the audience.

■ *Enunciate clearly.* Don't use words you're unfamiliar with and avoid verbal crutches, like "um" and "you know." Pronouncing words incorrectly or mumbling creates a poor impression.

■ *Smile.* A warm smile puts your audience at ease and helps you project self-confidence. But don't project a forced joviality either; that will turn an audience off. And if you're overly serious, you may come across as humorless and tense.

Try not to overprepare. We heard of one salesperson, for example, who had 36 slides developed for various presentations and decided they were so good that he used *all* of them when making a presentation to one client. Two-and-a-half hours later, when his presentation was finally over, he was mortified when he asked for feedback from his audience and the president of the company responded dryly, "Next time, fewer slides please."

Also avoid memorizing your presentation and overrehearsing. Reciting a written speech word for word often sounds cold, and gestures that are too practiced look merely mechanical. Your best approach: Be yourself. If you really believe in your company and product, your sincerity and natural enthusiasm will register with the audience and act as a powerful endorsement for what you have to say.

Finally, prepare answers to questions that you think your audience might ask. Anticipate and plan for every possible thing that could go wrong. Just before you deliver your presentation, check your equipment and visual aids, if you are using them. Make certain everything is functioning properly, and have a backup plan.

More Tips

■ *Select the right presentation strategy.* Every audience is different. What works well with one customer may not succeed with another. Select a presentation strategy that will be effective for each audience you address and that will elicit a positive response. For example, if you're presenting to an entire department, you might want to use an approach that relies strongly on visuals. If you're presenting to a small group of decision makers, however, you might want to try a more personal, interactive approach. When presenting to executive-level groups, always focus on strategic, "big picture" issues.

> Attitude is key. The other skills can be gained and developed over time, but the right attitude has to be there from the beginning.

■ *Be creative.* No matter who your audience is, you'll want to make sure that your presentation is engaging and compelling. Use your imagination! Create visuals and handouts that are colorful and exciting. Incorporate rhetorical questions to add drama to what you say and to stimulate participation. Quote well-known or highly respected sources to increase your credibility and make your points memorable.

> Top salespeople have a good attitude. They're always enthusiastic. They think about the situation and often turn a problem into an opportunity.

■ *Use humor judiciously.* Humor can be an effective ice-breaker and helps to get your audience to relax and become more receptive to your message. Make sure that the humor you use is appropriate to a business setting: Don't tell ethnic, sexist, or racist jokes. Avoid sensitive social issues and off-color remarks. And stay away from long-winded stories. If you get nervous, you may forget the punch line, and end up looking more foolish than if you flubbed a one-liner.

■ *Offer your audience something new.* Make the meeting time worthwhile for your audience by providing them with new knowledge or information they can use—about their own industry, about their competitors, or about the marketplace in general. That way, even if they decide against accepting your recommendation, they'll continue to think highly of you as a business professional and may invite you back again in the future. One client put it aptly: "I expect the salesperson to be a professional businessperson who happens to be involved in selling."

■ *Take charge.* If you feel the meeting is going sour, "flip on the lights" and take charge. Probe to find out where the customer wants to take the discussion. Above all, don't give up, don't get defensive, and don't lose your sense of humor. Sometimes even the most seasoned presenters have an off day and make mistakes. In the end, remember that we're still just people doing business with other people.

BASIC SKILLS

All alligators are born with the innate ability to navigate through the muddy waters. We use our mouths to get what we want because our eyes and ears don't work so well. We show our pearly whites to communicate how great we are and what we have to offer. We lull our prey into bathing in the sun and wait for the right moment to bite. Sometimes it works and sometimes it doesn't. If we wait long enough, we're bound to get a nibble—sooner or later.

When properly honed and reinforced, the skills that differentiate the successful salesperson from the competition remain constant. With the right skills, the successful salesperson can make things happen. He or she can analyze accounts and prospects, create strategies to move the sales cycle forward, and manage every aspect of the sales process. As an expert, the skilled salesperson is constantly observing, communicating, and evaluating the situation.

Good skills help you make the best use of your time and the customer's. They help you conduct sales calls in a way that leads to informed, mutually beneficial decisions, and help you build strong, long-term business relationships. With good basic skills, you're better able to facilitate an open exchange with the customer and ensure understanding and agreement throughout the sales process. Selling skills help you to:

- Get the sales call off to a positive start.
- Set a clear direction for the call.
- Establish a positive climate in which you and the customer can talk freely.
- Talk about your product or service in a way that's meaningful to the customer.
- Respond effectively to customer concerns.
- End the sales call with clear and appropriate commitments.

The real challenge is to have the right mix of technical knowledge and selling skills. When you have those two things balanced properly, that's where you have success. Above all, good selling skills help you to get to know your customer better and clearly understand your customer's needs. By doing so, you're able to align yourself more closely with the customer and provide better solutions to the customer's problems.

We knew of one salesperson, for example, who worked for a big-name computer company and possessed exceptional product knowledge and technical expertise. But with little formal training in sales, he had a great deal of trouble applying what he knew to helping customers achieve their goals. Only after taking a comprehensive course in basic selling skills—learning how to probe effectively, listen actively, and uncover customer needs—did he become adept at closing sales and meet his revenue targets.

Salespeople need a variety of skills to succeed in selling today. These include:

> **Top salespeople have the capacity to gather, understand, and analyze a customer's business. Top salespeople have lots of customer information, and they close more easily.**

- *Analytical skills*—to recognize that a sales opportunity exists, to uncover and identify customer needs, and to assess how products or services can be applied to help the customer.

- *Communication skills*—to probe effectively, listen actively, and present ideas powerfully and persuasively.

- *People skills*—to establish rapport with the customer, "read" the signals the customer sends, and react appropriately.

- *Negotiation skills*—to discuss differences with the customer, compromise, and bring about mutually satisfying agreements.

- *Organizational skills*—to plan and organize the sales process and make sure goals are achieved.

By learning, practicing, and becoming proficient in these basic skills, salespeople can achieve better results more efficiently, without wasting time or resources.

STOP TALKING AND START LISTENING

Alligator Trap
To Get What You Want, Open Your Mouth

Alligators know that they are blessed with a big mouth for one reason only: to satisfy their unceasing appetite. There's no subtlety involved when it comes to devouring their next meal. Good salespeople can't be so obvious. They have to lure their customers with more than just their presence; they need top-notch skills.

Effective listening, an active exercise, is one of the most critical skills of a successful salesperson. Good listeners project themselves into the mind of the customer in an effort to better understand the customer. They listen not only for facts, but also for the meanings and feelings behind the facts. One customer told us about a salesperson who, once she gets started, is like trying to stop a train. After awhile, the customer isn't even hearing her and keeps thinking how to politely get this salesperson out of his office.

Active listening involves drawing out and mentally summarizing as much relevant information as possible so that you and the customer can work together to make sound business decisions.

OVERCOME BARRIERS TO LISTENING

Top salespeople don't just *hear* what their customers say, they *listen* actively to their customers. Active listening is not simply an automatic physiological response, but a mental effort to overcome any barriers that may interfere with listening to and understanding customers.

> Top salespeople listen. They focus on what the customer feels is important. If they don't listen, they don't know what the customer needs, and then they try to sell what they think the customer needs.

Just as you have to resist distractions and overcome *external* barriers to listening (e.g., ringing phones, office chatter, interruptions), you also have to overcome any *internal* barriers to listening, such as your own biases, your assumptions about the customer, or any immediate judgments based on how the customer looks, dresses, or speaks.

To become an active listener, you have to put aside whatever prejudices or preconceptions you may have about the customer. Don't let your personal feelings about the customer get in the way and avoid assuming that the customer's needs fit a certain profile. Just because two of your customers are in the same industry, for example, doesn't mean they have the same strategic needs or business objectives.

When you don't listen actively, you may make assumptions about the customer's needs or goals that aren't true, and you may focus on issues that aren't priorities for the customer. This can waste time and cause you to make recommendations that aren't mutually beneficial.

LISTEN FOR CLUES

Before it's appropriate for you to share information about your product or service, you have to listen to learn what's important to the customer, what the customer needs, and how you might help. To do that, listen attentively for any verbal clues that may reveal the customer's needs, such as:

- *I want. . . , I need. . . , or I hope. . .*
- *It's important to us that. . .*
- *Our objective is. . .*
- *What we're looking for is. . .*

When you feel you've heard the customer express a real problem or need, check for the accuracy of what you've heard by restating the facts in your own words. But don't jump to any conclusions while the customer is speaking. Later, you can evaluate this information and use it in your analysis of how you can help the customer.

> *"I don't begin to make a recommendation until I fully analyze the data I've gathered about the client."*

Also be alert to any nonverbal clues that may indicate what the customer is feeling while he or she talks: the tone and quality of the customer's voice, any long silences or pauses, and the customer's posture and body language. When nonverbal clues seem to contradict what the customer says, it's important for you to clarify the *meaning* of the customer's statements.

IDENTIFY AREAS TO PROBE

Active listening encourages the customer to continue speaking, and it sets the stage for effective probing. Probing creates a more productive exchange of information between you and the customer, and it provides the groundwork to move the sale forward. An added bonus: When you listen attentively to customers, they're often more motivated to cooperate and listen to you.

The salesperson who's too busy figuring out what to say next and how to respond often misses the customer's point—and may even derail the conversation. Research shows that once the listener makes a negative or positive response, the speaker tends to clam up and halt the discussion. If this happens during a sales call, you may miss out on valuable information the customer could reveal, including:

- *Concerns*—issues or problems the customer feels are important.
- *Attitudes*—how the customer feels about you, your organization, or your competitors.
- *Immediate and long-term needs*—what the customer wants to achieve or improve.
- *Decision makers*—others in the customer's company who may influence the sale.

Sometimes, one listening misstep can even cause you to lose a sale. We know one customer representative in banking who said he lost out on a simple refinancing loan because he didn't pick up on the customer's critical short-term needs. "He said he wanted to save $7,000 in interest payments, so I set up a three-year plan that would help him to meet that goal. But what I failed to understand was that he needed the money right away, so he ended up going to somebody else for the loan."

Listening actively helps you to gain the customer's confidence and respect and earn the right to ask the kinds of questions that will give you a clear and complete understanding of the customer's needs. It also sets the stage for the next step in the communication process, where you can discover how to put the information you've learned to good use.

The information you gain from listening actively to customers might be important to various departments within your own organization (e.g., to develop new products, design new packaging, and launch new ad campaigns). As a salesperson from a nonprofit organization indicated, "A nonprofit organization relies on reputation and relationships to remain viable in a dynamic environment. The overall success of its strategies and vision depends as much on effective listening skills to further internal development as it does on external results reflecting its public performance."

> Salespeople always needed to know their product, but they didn't really need to know the customer. Now they need to know how the product meets the needs of the customer.

More Tips

■ *Be interested rather than interesting.* Too many salespeople try to impress their customers by overpowering them with information, by trying to anticipate their needs, or by dominating the conversation. A better approach: Stop trying to hog the stage. Show that you're interested in what the customer has to say by paraphrasing, by asking pertinent questions, and by letting the customer determine the length and pace of the conversation.

■ *Strike an attentive pose.* Listening requires self-discipline and concentration, and it helps if you take an active posture. Lean forward in your chair, nod regularly to indicate your understanding, and look the customer in the eye when he or she is talking. If you sit up straight and assume the pose of an attentive listener, chances are you'll really become one.

- *Take notes.* The best time to analyze an account begins immediately after your meeting takes place. To make sure you have all the facts you need for your analysis, take notes when you talk to customers. Jot down any key words or ideas and impressions of the customer that you feel may prove important. Make notes of both the hard facts (financial numbers, stated needs) and the soft facts (what the customer cares about). Just after the call, review your notes and add your impression of what happened and why. When you've had a chance to reflect on what was said, review the key issues with your colleagues or manager.

5
LESSON

UNCOVER NEEDS AND GOALS

Alligator Trap
Not Learning Your Territory Well

"Today the art of selling is in gathering the facts, not in making the close."

Alligators don't want to take the time to get to know their swamp. They assume their prey is waiting, at their disposal. Good salespeople have to use their communication skills, however, to learn more before attempting to enter murky waters.

As a salesperson, you must be educated about your customer and the customer's business and strategic goals before you introduce solutions through your product. Understanding the customer's "big picture" helps you to avoid making wrong assumptions. It enables you to build bridges between your customer's needs and your organization's products and services.

The prospective customer must be guided—through effective probing—into realizing what he or she needs, as well as the value in dealing with a particular salesperson.

Don't tell your customer what his or her needs are. Ask questions to establish needs that you both recognize. Request permission to probe if you need to, and tell the customer why you must have the information. Never interrogate the customer with a barrage of ongoing questions, or with questions that may appear invasive or forward. Some customers may not want to talk about their needs and issues, so you have to be able to ask questions in a way that will get answers and build trust.

When it's appropriate in the sales interaction, discuss how your product or service can solve your customer's specific needs. Always focus on what's good for both the organization and for the individual. A top salesperson will make customers feel like he or she has their best interests in mind.

INTERVIEW FOR UNDERSTANDING

When you understand the full range of your customer's needs, you're in a much better position to provide a comprehensive, long-term solution that truly helps the customer. By addressing customer needs effectively, you gain the customer's trust and respect, and an edge in uncovering new selling opportunities.

The best way to uncover customer needs is through effective interviewing, which can only begin after you have first established rapport with the customer and made sure that customer feels comfortable disclosing business information. By asking the right questions, salespeople can direct the conversation to focus on the customer's priorities and interests; establish the customer's level of satisfaction with current products, services, or suppliers; or help the customer identify needs the customer wasn't aware of.

Here's an example of how this can work. One Virginia company that manages retirement communities had invited a salesperson from a major health care provider to deliver a presentation on supplemental mental health care programs. Though the company made it clear at the start that it was not interested in scrapping its basic indemnity plan, the salesperson was able to eventually sign it on to an HMO package with a managed mental health care component. How did the salesperson do it? By asking questions about premium hikes, the results of membership surveys, and changes in utilization rates, the salesperson uncovered considerable dissatisfaction with the existing plan and the need to replace it with a more cost-effective plan that offered employees a greater number of attractive network features.

When interviewing customers, ask the kinds of questions that help to develop a clear, complete, and mutual understanding of the customer's needs.

- A *clear* understanding means that for each need you know exactly what the customer wants and why it's important.

- A *complete* understanding means you know all of the customer's needs and how they rank in importance.

- A *mutual* understanding means that you and the customer share the same understanding of the customer's needs.

Effective interviewing also helps you to distinguish between an opportunity and a need. An opportunity may be a dissatisfaction the customer has or a new direction for the company. A need is a definite desire where you can help. Once you've identified a need, then you can position yourself as a resource for the customer—an ally who has an exclusive solution.

PROBE CONSULTATIVELY

Successful salespeople probe consultatively to gain a full understanding of the customer's needs. Effective probes involve the customer in the conversation and promote an open dialogue.

Top salespeople ask good probing questions, ask the right follow-up questions, and ask the kinds of questions that will get customers to talk.

Developing a clear understanding of customer needs requires a structured approach for gathering information, one that make use of both *open* and *closed* probes during the interview.

- *Open probes yield information for the salesperson.* They often begin with words and phrases that encourage a free response: How. . . ? Why. . . ? and Tell me more. . .

- *Closed probes confirm understanding and gain closure for the salesperson.* They often begin with words and phrases that limit a response: Do you. . . Have you. . . How many. . . ? Is it true that. . . ?

Using a mix of probes helps you to learn about the customer's company—its strategies and business goals, its culture and management processes, its challenges and opportunities. By using probes effectively, you can learn:

Ask open questions for a lot of information, closed questions for details and confirmation.

- *Valuable background information.* What does the company make or sell? What customers does the company market to? Who are the company's chief competitors?

- *Why the customer has a need.* What are the circumstances that prompted the customer to meet with you? What does the customer want to achieve or improve? What are the customer's business objectives?

- *Who your customer's customers are.* What internal customers does your customer have to satisfy? What roles do these people play in the customer's organization? What are the needs of these behind-the-scenes people?

- *The need behind the need.* Does the customer's expressed need stem from a greater or more basic need? What are the strategic needs behind the expressed need?

- *How needs are changing.* How has the customer's business changed in recent years? What new markets does the customer sell to? What new competitors does the customer face?

Try to avoid the overuse of open and closed probes, however. When you rely exclusively on open probes, your conversation may lack focus or direction. When you rely exclusively on closed probes, the customer may begin to feel as though he or she is being interrogated and may become unwilling to share critical information.

> Salespeople must constantly keep track of the customer's situation and how it has changed, and what the customer wants to do about it. They can't assume that the customer's situation is stable and that their needs stay the same.

CONFIRM YOUR UNDERSTANDING

Throughout the interaction, you should clarify the information you gather so that you are sure you understand it, and confirm your understanding of the customer's needs

> Now we think of everyone in the customer's company as being our customer. In the past, we only thought of the decision maker as the customer.

and goals. If necessary, restate what you've learned in your own words.

Confirming your understanding ensures that you and the customer achieve a mutual understanding. It allows you to move the sales cycle forward. It helps you to be certain that the customer does in fact have a need (and that you're not simply making assumptions), even if the customer hasn't expressed a need. At the end of the sales call, summarize what the customer has said to ensure that you're both on the same wavelength. Remember: Top salespeople never stop asking the customer questions and confirming their understanding.

More Tips

- *Establish multiple needs.* To make sure you uncover *all* the selling opportunities that may exist with a customer, don't limit yourself to your primary contact. Ask for the names of other prospects within the company, set up appointments to interview them, and then analyze their problems. How do their goals differ from those of your primary contact? What problems do they have in improving efficiency, bottom-line results, or customer loyalty? How can your product or service satisfy their needs?

- *Keep the customer talking.* To get the customer to open up to you—and reveal important business information—it's your responsibility to keep the conversation going. One way to do that: Try to view the customer more as a friend or colleague, and conduct the meeting in a relaxed and informal manner. One customer remarked that a top salesperson was more like a colleague than a salesperson. Talking with the salesperson was like having a conversation in the living room with your best friend. When customers feel that way they're much more likely to exchange critical information.

■ *Avoid technical jargon.* Conversation between a salesperson and customer is most productive when the salesperson uses words that are familiar to the customer. When you try to impress customers with technical jargon, big words, or complex business concepts, they can become defensive or feel threatened. To grease the wheels of conversation, keep your language clear and simple.

■ *Practice good diction.* To make sure that customers understand what you say, you have to express your ideas clearly. That means using the right language: Choose words that say what you mean, pronounce them correctly, and watch your grammar. The best salespeople practice good diction on the telephone and in face-to-face meetings with customers.

> If you have the intellect but can't communicate so that people understand you and act on what you say, you're going nowhere.

ALIGN WITH THE CUSTOMER

Alligator Trap
Closing in on Your Prey Too Quickly

Alligators often assume that they can hook a prospect and reel him or her in right away. But the reality is that prospects and customers must be comfortable with the pace of the sale and be reassured that a salesperson is on their side. They need to feel that they can trust the salesperson, and that they're dealing with a partner, not just a vendor.

To partner successfully with customers, a salesperson has to view the needs and goals from the customer's perspective and collaborate with them to develop creative solutions to their business problems. When you and the customer work

> Align with your prospect. Help the prospect realize that you are on the same team. Be on the prospect's side of the table and walk slowly up the ladder together.

together as a team, the result is a solution that matches the customer's needs and goals.

If you don't understand your customer's needs—and are not able to position your product or service to satisfy them—then the customer may feel that you're only interested in pushing what you have to sell and may doubt your commitment to the relationship.

LOOK THROUGH THE CUSTOMER'S GLASSES

Today's customers expect a lot from the salesperson. They expect you to align closely with them and to act as a trusted advisor and consultant. They expect you to be pleasant to work with and to care about them.

To align successfully with the customer, you have to:

- *Be interested in the customer.* Learn everything you can about the customer's business and industry. Show a genuine interest in helping the customer become more profitable, more productive, and more efficient.

- *Empathize with the customer.* Ask yourself: What would I do if I were in the customer's shoes? How would I feel if I were responsible for solving the customer's problems?

> Top salespeople see the problems that the customer has, they show him solutions, and they tie it all back to high priority needs.

- *Be there for the customer.* Maintain regular contact with the customer to stay informed of new developments in the customer's organization. Show that you're committed to providing ongoing service and that you're always available for the customer.

TEAM UP WITH THE CUSTOMER

Aligning with the customer means that you and the customer are working on the same team. You're both committed to maintaining the relationship, to promoting the customer's short- and long-term success, and to making mutually beneficial business decisions.

To team up successfully with a customer, you have to demonstrate a willingness to cooperate, to compromise, and to share responsibility. You have to:

■ *Resolve issues openly and honestly.* If you're experiencing problems with the customer, be willing to discuss them. Be diplomatic, of course, but say what's on your mind so that you can clear the air and move on.

■ *Pitch in.* Help the customer whenever you can. For example, if the customer has to deliver a presentation or make an internal sale, volunteer to share your expertise: Create slides, offer constructive criticism, or provide moral support by sitting in.

■ *Deliver on your promises.* Prove to customers that you're completely dependable. Always do what you say you're going to do, make sure delivery schedules and quality requirements are consistently met, and try to meet the customer's emergency needs.

> The most important thing is that customers know they can depend on me and that I will not let them down.

DELIVER EFFECTIVE SOLUTIONS

Above all, aligning yourself with the customer means working hard to find effective solutions to customer problems and to meeting customer needs. Helping your customer's business to grow and to prosper is the key to cultivating long-term, profitable partnerships.

To deliver effective solutions and meet the customer's needs, you have to show clearly how your product or

Salespeople have to develop an increased awareness for problematic situations. They need to ask themselves, What special solutions can I offer to the customer?

We are interested in building much longer term relationships now than in past years. We used to have suppliers who were in and out and then back again. Now, once in, they stay in as long as they can perform.

service can benefit the customer and provide value. You have to:

- *Translate features into benefits.* Features are characteristics of your product or service. Benefits describe what the features mean to the customer. To make sure the customer understands the value of the help you provide, describe the benefits of your product's features and gain the customer's agreement on their value.

- *Synthesize solutions.* Be creative when developing solutions to complex customer problems. For example, would a mix of products and services solve the problem better? Or would joining forces with another supplier (one who isn't in competition with you) help you to meet the customer's needs more fully?

- *Adapt and customize, when necessary.* There's no universal product for all customers or for any one customer's total needs. Tailor your product or service to every customer situation, if possible. Customers tend to favor suppliers who create solutions that are customized specifically for them.

Remember: Creating an alignment benefits both you and your customers. It allows you to develop the stable, long-term relationships that are generally more profitable for your sales organization. And it gives your customers the opportunity to work with a trusted supplier who has their best interests in mind.

More Tips

■ *Understand the customer mind-set.* To develop a better understanding of the customer mind-set, role-play with others in your organization. Pretend you're the customer to see how you feel when a salesperson tries to "reel you in" too quickly. Or have a colleague try to sell you a product or service; then, think of all the reasons why you shouldn't buy.

■ *Align selling and buying processes.* Top salespeople believe there's a "best way" to connect to the customer—that customers have a preferred way of buying—and they adjust their sales approach accordingly. For example, though you might like to fully understand customer needs before proposing a solution that also demonstrates your technical expertise, your customer may prefer that you "earn the right" to explore his or her circumstances by demonstrating what you know up front. Remember, any lack of alignment between the way you sell and the way the customer buys could end up costing you the sale.

> Everything starts with your customers. You need to understand what they want. To know, you have to put yourself in their shoes because sometimes they don't even know what they need.

- *Conduct a dry run.* To improve your effectiveness at translating features into benefits for the customer, practice verbalizing your responses to customers. Before making a presentation, conduct a dry run. Practice turning features into benefits, and become comfortable making benefit statements that address the customer's needs. Come up with some questions the customer might ask, and then practice how you'd respond to those questions.

- *Turn down business, if necessary.* If the product or service you offer doesn't adequately meet the customer's needs, admit it and walk away from the business. You might even recommend another supplier who *can* meet those needs. The credibility you gain in doing what's right for the customer will pay off in the long run by demonstrating your sense of professionalism and commitment. One businessperson states that if a top salesperson doesn't want to satisfy all of our needs, or can't do so, he or she should admit it.

> Be patient, don't rush. Acknowledge the customer's need, establish value, and reinforce benefits.

- *Be patient with customers.* You can't expect to establish solid business partnerships overnight. You have to work especially hard with some customers to overcome doubts and suspicions or any residual negative feelings they may harbor about salespeople. Don't become impatient with customers. Keep in mind that most selling is a process and, unlike transactional sales, involves a series of ongoing interactions, each one moving the customer closer to a commitment and to establishing the trust needed to build a long-term relationship.

7

CLOSE THE SALE

Alligator Trap
Basking in the Sun Too Long

Alligators enjoy hanging out in the swamp so much that sometimes they forget why they're there. Good salespeople enjoy the sales process but also know how to take the next step to secure the deal. Closing is the skill of gaining a commitment from the customer. It is one of the most important skills in the successful salesperson's repertoire; it can sometimes make up for an inferior presentation.

> Ask for a commitment; sometimes we forget.

Depending on the length of your selling cycle, closing may mean achieving the objective you set for a sales call, not necessarily making the final sale. The commitment you receive from the customer might be an agreement to buy or simply an interim agreement. To review a proposal, attend a demonstration or involve other decision makers in upcoming meetings.

Commitment and closure come only after all customer issues have been addressed effectively during the call and you've won the customer's confidence. Before asking for a commitment, always confirm the customer's understanding of the issues involved. Beware of moving to close too quickly! Don't be aggressive and force the customer to close, or become obnoxious by pushing the value of your product and its "obvious" superiority over those of your competitors. If you move too quickly, the customer may doubt your commitment to understanding and satisfying his or her needs.

FORMULATE AN ACTION PLAN

Each sales call you make with a customer should help you advance the sale and move to a final close. The objective you set for each call should guide you in pursuing the kind of commitments you seek from the customer.

To help you set appropriate objectives for your sales calls, formulate a logical action plan in a sequence that moves the customer comfortably toward making a final commitment. At the end of each call, try to gain the best commitment you can from the customer.

But don't become discouraged if you don't achieve your primary objective for each call. Establish alternative objectives for each call, and strive to achieve at least one of these objectives. Remember, it's the relationship, not the sales call, that leads to a sale.

Planning is critical. Football teams don't win by accident.

KNOW WHEN TO CLOSE

Ask for a customer commitment only at the appropriate time— when you've done a good job of probing, exchanged information about the customer's needs, and shown how your product or service can help meet those needs. Then the customer and you are ready to make a decision about how to close the sales call and what steps should be taken next.

Top salespeople have an idea of what they want to bring to the table. Then they listen well enough, so that they know when the time is right to position it. One of the best times to close is when you get a clear signal of the customer's readiness to commit. The signals that salespeople may "read" from the customer include:

- A smile, nod, or expectant look from the customer.
- A clear statement of customer satisfaction, such as "That sounds like just what we're looking for."
- A statement that shows the customer wants to close the call, such as "What's the next step?" or "How should we proceed now?"
- Customer questions about delivery time, costs, terms and conditions, or product support.

When the customer sends out these signals, don't go on to discuss other things and miss the key moment to ask for a commitment.

KNOW HOW TO CLOSE

When you feel the time is right to ask for a customer commitment, close the call:

- *Recap what's been discussed.* Summarize the benefits of your product or service that the customer has already accepted and reinforce its value in meeting the customer's needs.
- *Check for remaining concerns.* Don't close until you're sure you've responded to all the customer's objections or concerns, and that the customer is satisfied with your responses.

> **The salesperson must have the capacity and the intellect to absorb a tremendous amount of information, and then turn it into action that yields results.**

■ *Close on the commitment.* Make a statement that clearly reflects the customer's commitment. Example: "So it's agreed that we'll proceed with the first stage of implementation, and then evaluate results after three months."

Throughout the close, use language that reflects that an agreement has been reached. Don't express doubt, hesitancy, or uncertainty, and always demonstrate that you value the relationship through your words and actions. Smile at the customer or shake the customer's hand. Positive, confident behavior inspires the same attitude in your customer and communicates trustworthiness.

If you can't get the customer to make a decision or to commit, try to get a date by which a decision or commitment could be made. Above all, don't close the call if it doesn't feel right. Trust your instincts!

When asked about the right time to ask for a commitment, one salesperson said, "I can't explain it, but I know it."

REVIEW NEXT STEPS

Following the commitment, gain agreement with the customer on what has to be done next to ensure that the commitment is carried out. The reviewing process accomplishes several goals:

■ You help the customer understand what he or she has to do to move the process forward.

- You demonstrate your commitment to working with the customer.
- You emphasize the mutuality of the commitment.

Always check for acceptance from the customer, to make sure the customer is willing to do whatever is involved in carrying out the commitment. If the customer suggests a next step that's unreasonable or impossible for you to carry out:

- Ask the customer to explain why he or she wants you to take that next step.
- Explain the difficulty or problems you see in taking that step.
- Propose an alternate step that would benefit the customer, or suggest modifications in the timing or conditions for taking the step the customer has suggested.

As difficult as it is sometimes to gain commitment from customers, remember that in the end your real challenges *begin* with the commitment, which signals the possibility of a long-term relationship. How well you and the customer carry out the commitment—and the efforts you make along the way to nurture the relationship—will have a big impact on your ability to build a long-term partnership.

It's necessary to establish a trust-oriented relationship between the salesperson and the customer—one that goes beyond simply buying and selling.

More Tips

- *Always ask for referrals.* When you commit yourself to helping your customers succeed, your customers will often respond in kind. If they respect you as a sales professional and appreciate your efforts on their behalf, they're usually willing to help you gain more business even if they don't buy your product or service themselves. So every time you conclude a selling cycle with a customer, ask for referrals to other people in the customer's organization or other companies.

- *Don't trash your competitors.* Some salespeople try to make themselves look good in the eyes of their customers by putting down their competitors. Be careful: This strategy almost always backfires. In reality, customers are usually more receptive to you when you position the capabilities of your product or service honestly and don't focus on the failures of your competitors or on the shortcomings of their offerings.

> Real sales professionals are positive in their selling attitudes. They sell their product's intrinsic merits rather than the negatives of a competitor's product.

- *Keep in touch with customers.* Even when there's no prospect of an immediate sale, you should never abandon a customer. There might be other opportunities for you to work together in the future. What's more, the relationship you establish with the customer may help you gain referrals or recommendations. How can you maintain contact? Call the customer up occasionally, send along product information or industry reports that might interest the customer, and keep the customer up-to-date on new products or services you can offer and on changes in your own organization.

- *Conduct a postsale inventory.* Routinely update files and customer information at the end of every selling cycle. Whether or not you make the sale, always conduct a postsale inventory. Review what happened during the sales process—how the customer reacted to you, what the customer objected to, what commitments the customer was willing to make—and analyze what you could have done differently. If the sale was difficult or complex, ask a colleague or your sales manager to conduct the inventory with you.

> **Top salespeople are motivated by the intrinsic rewards more than the extrinsic ones. They're focused on the activity of selling, rather than on the income from it.**

■ *Learn from the experience.* Try to think of every new sale and customer as another opportunity to practice and improve your selling skills. Whenever possible, solicit feedback from your customers. This is especially valuable in helping you determine what you can do better next time. If you do win their business, ask customers what made them decide to buy or what they liked best about your selling style. If you don't get their business, ask why. By learning from your experience, you establish a process of continuous self-improvement that's bound to enhance your sales success.

THREE

BUYING ATTITUDES

My second cousin Sydney, from the Aussie outback, claims what's important to snagging customers down under is to antici-pate their actions and to have a strategy for handling them—but Sydney is a croc!

People say I'm just a creature from the swamp, but they're wrong. If my customer has an attitude, I'm not going to wrestle with him. Nor am I going to make a snap decision on how to act.

Sometimes, as my customer thrashes around in the murky waters, I lay low and let my little eyes skim—you know, pretend-ing to study the environment. I give him enough time to realize what's really good for him. If that doesn't work, I simply open my mouth wider and let him have it. He stops complaining real soon.

Alligators may turn a deaf ear to the attitudes of their customers, but a good salesperson can't afford such arro-gant behavior. As our research shows, customers these days are more sophisticated, more knowledgeable, and more demanding than ever before. Customer priority is causing their businesses to grow, and plenty of resources are available in the marketplace to help customers succeed. As one salesperson recently told us in our study of buying behaviors, "Golf games and friendships don't guarantee customer loyalty anymore." If you're in sales today, you must continually earn the right to do business with customers.

> Customers are looking for someone to make their business more profitable.

To establish yourself as a resource for the customer, you must demonstrate your knowledge of the customer's immediate and long-term goals, problems, and needs. And you must be sensitive to the customer's culture and ways of doing business. "Not only do our people have to possess more business and industry knowledge than ever before," a sales manager in our study commented, "they also have to be able to articulate what they know and relate it to the customer's situation."

> The days of simply walking in and selling your product are over.

A customer's attitude toward you and what you sell generally falls into one of three categories: positive, neutral, or negative. Even when customers are receptive to you and have real needs to discuss, they may not be satisfied with the solution you offer them or with certain aspects of your product or service. They may express a variety of concerns that will have to be resolved before you can move ahead with the sale.

Other customers may seem neutral or indifferent about doing business with you. They may not realize that they have needs that you can satisfy. They may not know your organization or about your product or service.

Negative attitudes reflect real customer concerns and are the most difficult to overcome. They may indicate that the customer dislikes doing business with you or your company, feels your product or service can't satisfy organizational needs, or has serious doubts that you can really help.

Many factors can influence a customer's attitude:

- *Previous experience with your organization.* The customer may have dealt with another salesperson from your organization in the past, and that experience has colored the customer's current attitude.

- *Industry gossip or hearsay.* The customer may have heard certain things about you or your organization from co-workers or colleagues, which may have biased the customer's attitude.

- *Organizational characteristics.* The customer may have so much work that he or she doesn't have time for you, may be experiencing organizational pressures (e.g., to cut costs or increase profits), or may be committed to working with other suppliers.

- *Personal characteristics.* The customer may be unfriendly by nature, closed-minded, or resistant to change; may be difficult to work with in general; or may simply dislike salespeople.

> At first, you have to treat all customers with kid gloves until you know how far you can go, how they'll react in a given situation, which products they want or don't want, and which companies they've worked closely with in the past.

There are times when you won't be clear about the customer's attitude. He or she may be difficult to "read," may attempt to hide negative feelings by stalling, or may send you mixed signals.

In those situations, it's necessary to ask questions or probe to gain a clear understanding of the customer's attitude before attempting to address it. To do otherwise—or to guess about the customer's attitude—would be risky. You may attempt to move forward with a sale without completely resolving the customer's concerns. You may overlook the drawbacks that a customer sees in your product or service. Or you may end up wasting your time on a customer who remains indifferent to you.

Dealing with customer attitudes requires effective strategies, clear communication, and expert selling skills. They can help you reinforce positive customer attitudes, overcome neutral or negative attitudes, and enhance your efforts to establish long-term, mutually beneficial customer partnerships.

> **Top salespeople make the right judgment about the kind of customers they're dealing with and know what's going on with them. They know when the time is right to sell something and when it's not right.**

8

OVERCOME INDIFFERENCE

Alligator Trap
Only Seek a Sure Thing

Alligators don't have time for indifference. Either you're in or you're out. After all, it's a jungle out there. But good salespeople aren't afraid of a challenge nor are all customers willing prey. Some need to be convinced that you have their best interests at heart.

Indifference is the most difficult customer attitude to overcome. It can be caused by many factors, including satisfaction with a competitive product or service, the perception that you sell a commodity with no unique benefits, unawareness of existing needs, or simply the inability of the customer to see that he or she can do better.

Customers demonstrate indifference in a variety of ways. They may try to put you off or repeatedly postpone a scheduled meeting. They may appear bored or inattentive during your meeting. Or they may openly express their indifference with "I'm sorry, but we're just not interested at this time."

Successful salespeople see indifference as a challenging opportunity to uncover unidentified needs or dissatisfaction. Instead of focusing on their product or service, successful salespeople always focus on the customer's situation and how it can be improved. However, you may not be able to plan all of your strategy beforehand; you have to follow the mood and reactions of the customer. Successful salespeople also know when walking away from the indifferent customer is not only acceptable, but the best use of their time.

ASK PERMISSION TO PROBE

When responding to customer indifference, first acknowledge the customer's viewpoint. Always reassure the customer that you won't take up much of his or her time, and that it's not your intention to sell something that's not needed.

> Don't burn your bridges on the current situation if the customer isn't interested. Share what you have to offer, and leave the door open for the future.

Then explore to determine if your timing was wrong. Perhaps a current contract with a competitor doesn't run out for another six months or you've missed the budgeting process. If either is true, ask when the time is right to call again—say, in three to six months—and try to get the customer to commit by scheduling an appointment.

If timing is not an issue, then request permission to probe. Try to position your probe as having value to the customer; for example, in the hope that you might be of service to the customer now or sometime in the future.

When requesting permission to probe, always be sure to limit your agenda in scope and time. Say something like, "If I could ask you a few brief questions, I might be able to give you some helpful suggestions" or "I'd like to ask you a couple of questions to see if there's a reason for us to continue meeting."

If the customer gives you permission to probe, then proceed to ask about the customer's current conditions or visions for the future, and seek out possible needs. Your objective is to get the customer to talk and provide information, and to identify any problems the customer might have. One salesperson says that she always tries to get them to talk about their company, because the more they talk, the more she can find out.

CREATE AWARENESS OF NEEDS

Probing with an indifferent customer provides an opportunity for you to explore any problems the customer might have with current suppliers, to discuss possible new strategies the customer is entertaining, or to review pressures the customer feels from competitors. Any of these could result in the customer realizing needs of which he or she was previously unaware.

When you probe to overcome indifference:

- *Find out about other suppliers.* With whom is the customer currently doing business? How satisfied is the customer with these suppliers? Is there anything the customer would change about these relationships?

- *Explore customer strategies and goals.* What are the customer's business objectives? Has the customer's organization changed its strategic direction? How can your product or service promote these new business goals?

- *Analyze the customer's competition.* Who are the customer's primary competitors? Is the customer losing or gaining market share? Are there any new rivals that threaten the customer's organization?

Another good probing strategy is to ask how the customer currently does something and how well that process or procedure is working out. Your objective is to uncover needs by helping the customer determine how satisfied he or she is with the way things are now. For example, you might ask:

> Very few people are completely satisfied with what they've got at the moment. There is always some area where you can provide them with something.

- How does doing things that way affect your business?
- How do you feel about the results you're now getting?
- What impact does that have on your customers? your quality? your productivity? your bottom line?

When you probe to establish the customer's level of satisfaction, you heighten the customer's awareness of the consequences of leaving things unchanged, and that may prompt the customer to recognize a need. Example: Suppose a salesperson asks a customer, "Are you satisfied with the phone system you have now?" The customer might respond, "We love it; everything seems to be fine." But if the salesperson follows up with a more penetrating probe—"You mean you haven't experienced any problems at all?"—it may stimulate the customer to undertake a more critical evaluation and recognize that change may carry some benefits.

Never try to introduce a customer need that the customer doesn't recognize and express. If you do, the customer might feel that you're simply pushing your product or service.

ADOPT A LONG-TERM VIEW

Short-term thinking is what separates the reptiles from the higher forms of life. Patience and persistence are the key to building a successful sales relationship. Don't expect to turn around an indifferent customer in one or two sales calls. It takes time for customers to change their thinking about what they need and to develop trust in a salesperson.

We know of one salesperson in the furniture rental business who spent two years trying to win over a large real estate firm that leased furnished apartments to business travelers. The firm was committed under a long-term contract to a competitor, but the salesperson's perseverance and interest were part of the reason the real estate firm decided to switch suppliers once the contract expired.

With an indifferent customer, it's sometimes necessary to develop a long-term perspective. Even when you can't make a sale or gain a commitment from the customer, the time you spend with an indifferent customer may still pay off. You may be able to:

- *Build rapport.* Introduce yourself and your company, and show the customer that you're interested in doing business.

- *Explain what you can offer.* Demonstrate your business knowledge and expertise, and offer yourself as a resource for the customer.

- *Build knowledge about the customer.* Use the opportunity to learn what you can about the customer and his or her company and industry—knowledge you may be able to apply to other selling situations.

- *Receive permission to come back.* Even if you can't make progress on your first meeting with the customer, you may at least receive permission to come back and try again. One salesperson said that he had to work harder to prove himself with newly established relationships. He would do something extra, such as bringing customers information on subjects that interest them.

You can't always be successful in making a sale to an indifferent customer, but don't let that stop you from trying to establish a relationship. Indifferent customers may provide useful information about other customers in the same industry or give you valuable references for new customers.

> Top salespeople weigh the decision if it is worth the time to pursue the indifferent customer and consider, "Is this the right thing for us to do? Is this profitable?"

How do you know when you *are* wasting your time? When you feel you're not getting an adequate return on the time, energy, and resources you invest in an indifferent customer, then it may be time to terminate the relationship and move on.

More Tips

■ *Learn to recognize indifference.* You'll begin to deal with customer indifference more effectively once you learn how to distinguish it from other customer buying attitudes (e.g., skepticism). Familiarize yourself with customer scenarios that suggest indifference. Analyze those accounts where indifference may exist, and determine why. Ask yourself: Have competitive suppliers established inroads with these types of customers or companies? Is my product or service unsuited to the companies in this industry?

> Top salespeople have a good attitude. They're always enthusiastic. They think around the situation and often turn a problem into an opportunity.

■ *Don't lose your cool.* Indifferent customers can sometimes be ungracious or abrupt—even rude—but their offputting demeanor doesn't mean you can't overcome their indifference. Working with the proper skills and attitudes (especially patience and perseverance), successful salespeople often secure sales from customers who were initially indifferent. So maintain your composure whenever you encounter indifference. Try not to focus on how the indifferent customer makes you feel but on what you can offer the customer and on your objective for the sales call.

> Where the differences between products are limited, salespeople must have the ability to be different and to be remembered.

■ *Differentiate yourself.* If the customer believes your product or service can be easily purchased elsewhere (and perhaps more cheaply), one way to stand out from your competition is to demonstrate the unique qualities, knowledge, or services that *you* can provide. Ask yourself: What can I do for this customer that my competitors can't? What unique expertise do I have to offer this customer?

9

ANTICIPATE OBJECTIONS

Alligator Trap
Wrestle with Those Who Challenge You

When an alligator encounters an objection, he's likely to rely on his muscles to have his way. Good salespeople have other techniques available to them. Usually they are more subtle, on the understanding that might seldom makes right.

Objections are a normal part of the sales process. Sometimes a customer's objections or concerns are valid; sometimes they're irrational or irrelevant. Real objections—not just excuses—are logical to the prospective customer, even if they are not to the salesperson.

It's important to remember that objections represent opportunities. They often suggest customer interest in what the salesperson has presented. When an objection is raised, the customer frequently is looking to you to clear up a misunderstanding, to provide additional information about your product or service, or to remove any remaining doubts about making the purchase.

Customers need more reassurance that they've made the right decision because the costs involved today are often very high.

You must become adept at handling objections on several fronts: when trying to set up a call, while conducting a presentation, when attempting to gain commitment, and sometimes even after a sales call. All objections should be answered sincerely, thoroughly, and with empathy.

Most objections fall under the categories of misunderstandings or drawbacks. The specific strategies for handling each of these types of objections are discussed in the following two lessons.

DEVELOP A POSITIVE ATTITUDE

Customers raise objections when they don't understand, accept, or agree with what you say. Though objections present challenges for salespeople, they also serve a useful purpose: They help to promote a productive dialogue between the customer and the salesperson.

Research shows that when you handle customer objections effectively, you make a better impression on the customer and you're more likely to make a sale. By resolving objections, you're also more likely to reach a mutually beneficial agreement with the customer.

A positive attitude is essential to responding effectively to objections. Though some salespeople look at objections in a negative way as major roadblocks to a sale, the most successful salespeople view them differently: as opportunities to enlighten the customer, to learn more about the customer, and to convince the customer of how they can help. One salesperson believes that objections are a good sign. They mean that the customer is interested, is tracking with her. Objections give her an opportunity to continue talking and to gather and provide more information.

Top salespeople learn to anticipate objections. They sometimes develop a list of responses to the most commonly raised objections. And they develop selling skills to deal successfully with objections.

ACKNOWLEDGE OBJECTIONS

We've learned several techniques from salespeople who are effective in resolving customer objections. First, whenever you encounter a customer objection, acknowledge it—don't ignore it. If the customer appears hesitant to raise an objection, try to draw the customer out. Ask, "Do you have any questions about what I've said so far?" or "Have I neglected to cover any issues that you consider important?"

If necessary, work with the customer to articulate any objections, so that you can respond to the objections. By dealing with customer objections proactively, you send the message that you're eager to do business with the customer and that you have his or her interests in mind.

I keep a list of objections I run into for each of the services I sell. Next to each one I jot down points to say or questions I need to ask. Sometimes asking the right questions helps me to understand the situation better.

Top salespeople are sensitive and perceptive. They have the ability to read what's on the other person's mind and verbalize it even before they say it.

Always demonstrate empathy with the customer by listening attentively to the customer's objection. Don't interrupt until the customer has fully explained the objection in his or her own words. Use the proper body language while the customer is talking to show that you're listening carefully, and then repeat the objection to make sure you fully understand it.

Once an objection has been raised, evaluate it to figure out where the customer is coming from: Is it indifference or is the customer just expressing a misunderstanding? For example, if the customer says, "We're perfectly satisfied with what we have now," you may be dealing with indifference. But if the customer says, "Your product just isn't up to our standards," the customer may misunderstand what your product can offer. Knowing what type of objection the customer has will help you develop an effective response.

PROBE TO CLARIFY

To clarify the objection, ask questions: "How do you feel about what I've just said?" "Is there anything more that you'd like to know?" "Do you think this will help to solve your problem?" Make sure that you:

- *Know what kind of concern the customer is expressing.* If the customer expresses a drawback about your product or service, you might want to emphasize other features and benefits. If the customer misunderstands something you've said, you may have to provide additional information or simply repeat what you said in a different way.

- *Understand the concern thoroughly.* Behind many customer objections are unexpressed or unidentified needs. By probing—or using questions systematically—you can uncover hidden needs, learn more information about the customer, and gain the opportunity to demonstrate how you can satisfy those needs.

■ *Allow the customer to fully express doubts or misgivings.* When customers are reluctant to express an objection, probing may help the customer to open up and say exactly what's on his or her mind. This fosters a better exchange of information between you and the customer, which helps to build a stronger business relationship. A salesperson we know asks: "What do you want to know? What would make you feel more comfortable?" These are not manipulative questions, but "seeking" questions.

When you feel you adequately understand the customer's concern, then provide the appropriate information to resolve it. Always check to make sure that the information you provide has been accepted by the customer and that the concern has been resolved to the customer's satisfaction. You might simply ask, "Does that satisfy all your concerns?" Then pay close attention to the customer's body language and facial expressions, and if you sense discomfort in the customer or continued concerns, say something like, "I get the feeling that you still have some reservations or doubts. Would you like me to walk through this again just to make sure we've covered everything to your satisfaction?"

More Tips

■ *Identify various types of objections.* The best way to deal with objections is to anticipate and prepare for them. Many top salespeople have a system for classifying objections, which they often share with their colleagues. To develop a typology of your own, compile a list of possible objections and the strategies you might use to respond to them. Think of all the objections that might arise in a particular customer situation, and then decide what you would do or say to completely resolve them.

■ *Respect the customer's honesty.* Don't assume that customers raise objections simply to be disagreeable or difficult. Most objections represent real customer concerns or questions the customer needs to have answered to defend the purchase decision within the company. So acknowledge the customer's right to raise objections and develop respect for the customer's honesty in doing so. This will help you to develop a more positive attitude toward objections, accept them as a normal part of the sales process, and become more patient with customers.

▪ *Don't enter into a debate.* Customer objections can sometimes make you feel defensive about your product or service, your organization, or yourself. Don't allow this emotional response to guide your actions; otherwise, you may adopt an adversarial stance with the customer and undermine rapport. When objections are raised, never enter into a debate with the customer to prove the customer wrong. Instead, focus on educating the customer by clearing up any misunderstandings, offering proof sources for what you say, or providing additional information on the features and benefits of your product.

RESOLVE MISUNDERSTANDINGS

Alligator Trap
Chew Them Up and Spit Them Out

When was the last time you saw alligators taking the time to sort things out? While efficient, their approach hardly attracts repeat business. Good salespeople can't be so cavalier; they need to address misunderstandings as they arise. However, simply clearing up the confusion and moving on to other issues is not always the best strategy. You must fully grasp the reasons behind the misunderstanding before you can resolve it. And you should use the misunderstanding as an opportunity to identify other customer concerns. Often clearing up one misunderstanding will draw out other concerns the customer might have—or reveal that a bigger problem exists.

Never treat a misunderstanding lightly. The way you handle a misunderstanding demonstrates your competence as a salesperson, your selling style, and your sense of professionalism. It shows the customer how important his or her concerns are to you, and it sends a message about how much you value the customer's business.

> Perception is the most critical challenge throughout a sale. Everyone perceives differently. It is your job to get inside the customer's head to understand his or her perception and to deal with it, so that the customer elects you over the competition.

LOOK FOR CAUSES

What accounts for misunderstandings? Reasons vary widely, including:

- *Incorrect or insufficient information.* The customer may have knowledge about you, your organization, or your product or service that's out of date, incomplete, or simply wrong.
- *Bad impressions.* You may have made a poor first impression on the customer. Or the customer's opinions may have been shaped by interactions with another salesperson from your organization or with other salespeople in general.
- *Unsatisfied needs.* The customer may have a need that you can satisfy but doesn't know it, often because the two of you haven't identified or discussed the need.

A misunderstanding can occur at any time in the selling cycle. Whenever you encounter one, ask questions to find out where the customer got the wrong idea. For example, did it stem from something you said or did? Were you unclear in how you expressed yourself? Was it based on something the customer read in an advertisement or company brochure? Did your competitors say something about you or your organization that's confused the customer? By pinpointing the source of the misunderstanding, you may be able to take action and make sure the same misunderstanding doesn't happen again with other customers.

USE A SYSTEMATIC APPROACH

The most effective strategy for dealing with misunderstandings is to use a three-step approach:

- Acknowledge the customer's viewpoint.
- Probe for a full understanding.
- Provide the appropriate information that will get you on the right track.

Often, a customer misunderstanding is based on a belief that you can't provide a certain product feature or benefit when in fact you can! In those situations, you may be able to clear up the misunderstanding simply by providing additional information to the customer, offering a proof source, or performing a demonstration.

For example, suppose a customer mistakenly assumes that your company requires a 50 percent down payment when buying your product, and refuses to lay out such a large sum up front. When the customer makes this objection, you might respond in this way: "I realize that you feel such a requirement is unreasonable, and you'd be perfectly justified in going to another supplier if that were the case. But let me assure you that it's not our policy to ask for a down payment from longstanding customers. Unlike most of our competitors, we offer an 18-month payment schedule with no interest to our established customers."

PROBE FOR HIDDEN NEEDS

At other times, misunderstandings can be traced to unexpressed or unidentified customer needs. In those cases, you'll want to probe to seek the need *behind* the misunderstanding, confirm the need, and then demonstrate how your product or service can meet this need.

Suppose the customer described above remains reluctant to close the deal, despite the offer of a long-term payment schedule. You might then probe for hidden needs by asking: "Do you still feel that the payment terms we're offering are unacceptable?" "What payment terms does your company usually agree to?" "How would you design a payment schedule that would be ideally suited to your company?" Through such questions you may discover, for example, that the customer's company is experiencing a severe but short-term cash flow problem. When you tell the customer that you can meet the need, be sure to identify the specific feature of your product or service that helps you to do that and demonstrate how it benefits the customer. You might say: "For special situations like this one, our flexible payment policy allows longtime customers to postpone making their first installment payment for up to three months. This will allow you to improve your productivity right away, without assuming an additional financial burden."

> More than ever, salespeople need to be able to uncover needs, address needs, and show how your products satisfy needs.

By confirming the customer's need, you help the customer look at the misunderstanding in a more positive light—as something the customer needs or wants—rather than as a problem, something that's wrong with your product or service.

Whatever the source of the misunderstanding, you should always check back with your customer for acceptance to ensure that the concern has been resolved completely and that no other misunderstandings need to be addressed.

More Tips

- *Never argue with the customer.* At times, customers may become defensive when you try to clear up a misunderstanding. They may not immediately accept the information or explanation you provide. However, trying to prove the customer wrong and arguing with the customer are not effective strategies; both can severely damage a business relationship. A better approach is to express yourself clearly and calmly to clear up the misunderstanding and, if necessary, tactfully rephrase your statements to make sure you get through to the customer. One salesperson puts the burden on herself for not being clear. She sometimes suggests walking through the issues again, so that the client doesn't feel defensive.

- *Never blame the customer.* Customers are sometimes the source of their own misunderstandings. When they listen to industry gossip, for example, or fail to read product literature thoroughly, they may develop misconceptions about your product or service or harbor prejudices that impede understanding. Still, you should never adopt an accusatory stance with a customer. Remember: It's your job to set the customer straight in the most professional manner possible and without casting blame.

> Top salespeople believe first of all in their product and show it.

- *Champion your product or service.* Besides logical reasoning, the enthusiasm you demonstrate for your product or service can also help correct a customer's misperceptions. When the customer sees how much you believe in what you sell, he or she is less likely to accept negative rumors or to form opinions based on incomplete or inaccurate information. Your commitment to your product or service can be a powerful force in shaping the customer's mind-set.

DEAL WITH DRAWBACKS

Alligator Trap
Alligators Don't Have Time for Obstacles

When an alligator senses the prey might be out of reach, its eyes immediately search the horizon for other opportunities. Good salespeople do just the opposite; they work to overcome selling obstacles such as drawbacks.

Drawbacks don't have to be showstoppers or deal breakers. Though drawbacks can have a significant impact on a potential sale, they don't have to derail the sale. Remember, customers make buying decisions based on how well you can satisfy their *overall* needs, not just a single isolated need.

Still, you should never ignore a drawback. When a customer says your product doesn't have the right features or that your price is higher than a competitor's, you should always acknowledge their complaint. That lets the customer know that you consider these concerns legitimate and that you want to satisfy the customer. Sometimes the customer doesn't think about the total cost, only the monthly payment.

If that's the case, that should tell the salesperson that he or she didn't find out enough about the customer's real need. If they have a real need and want to solve it, then price is not a critical factor.

The customer expectation today is that every deal should be the best deal.

The best way to resolve a drawback is to redirect the customer's focus to the "bigger picture." For example, let's say your customer likes everything about your product—a high-quality commercial copier—but objects to the hefty price tag. You might say, "You're definitely right that our copiers are more expensive than those of our competitors, but the quality we offer for that price can't be matched by any other supplier. And isn't quality what's most important to achieving your primary objective—improving service to your customers?"

ISOLATE THE DRAWBACK

Drawbacks occur during a sale when your product or service can't fully satisfy the customer. Drawbacks aren't uncommon, but you may not always be aware that they exist. Without telling you why, for example, a customer may respond to you with impatience or hostility, or try to stall the sale.

Whenever you suspect a drawback exists, probe to fully understand the customer's hesitancy or concern. First, make sure that you're not dealing with customer indifference or a misunderstanding. To ferret out the drawback, you might say:

> I get the feeling that you have some concerns about what I'm saying. Is it because you don't think you have a real need for our product? Is there anything about it that you don't understand?

Then, when it's clear that the customer is truly dissatisfied in some way with your product or service—that a drawback exists—acknowledge it. Say, "I understand that perhaps you're having difficulty with our warranty plan" or whatever the problem is.

> Salespeople need to apply their fact-finding skills not only in a straightforward way, but also to find out financial and economic information, which will probably be key decision factors.

Even if you don't agree with the customer's evaluation, never question the customer's logic or thinking; that may offend the customer. Instead, isolate the drawback to show that it's only one factor among many in the buying decision. Then try to resolve the drawback in a positive way by demonstrating the ways your product or service *can* satisfy the customer. You might say, "OK, we've established so far that the warranty we offer doesn't meet your requirements. But let's focus for a minute on some of the other features of our product and see how well they can help you achieve your productivity and quality goals."

FOCUS ON THE BIG PICTURE

When your product or service is not a perfect solution to the customer's problem, try to redirect the customer's attention to his or her "big picture" needs. This helps the customer to put the drawback in perspective and to view it in the context of other important needs. Your strategy might include the following questions:

- Does our product or service satisfy your most critical needs?

To make the right decision, salespeople are going to ask questions that are more penetrating, more subtle, and more carefully phrased.

- Compared to what you're using now, can our product or service do a better job for you *overall?*
- Are the advantages of using our product or service greater than the disadvantages?

If the customer and you agree that the need you can't satisfy is less important than other needs, it may be beneficial for you both to move forward with the sale. But don't put words in the customer's mouth. Always check for acceptance before moving on, and confirm the customer's agreement to proceed.

OUTWEIGH THE DRAWBACK

Another effective way to deal with a drawback is to outweigh it by reinforcing certain benefits of your product or service, especially those the customer has already accepted. These may include:

- Benefits that meet high-priority customer needs.
- Benefits that you know your competitors can't provide.
- Benefits that meet hidden or unidentified needs.

If the drawback still seems like a major obstacle to the customer, then request permission to continue probing; for example, say, "I understand that you refuse to buy a product that doesn't meet your warranty requirements. But may I ask you a few more questions before we end our discussion?" In such cases, you'll often uncover information that makes the customer aware of additional needs, many of which you can satisfy with your product or service.

Resolving drawbacks is a critical part of the sales process and an important step to reaching mutually beneficial agreements. It helps you to reinforce the benefits you can offer the customer, and it helps the customer to look at things differently and assess which needs are most important. The quote on this page illustrates how a drawback was resolved.

More Tips

- *Walk in the customer's shoes.* A good way to learn how to deal effectively with drawbacks is to try to experience how the customer feels about them. Pretend you're a customer and, with another salesperson from your organization, role-play a situation in which you're faced with the decision of buying a product that doesn't satisfy all your needs. How do you feel about having to choose an imperfect solution? How do you feel about buying a product or service that has drawbacks?

Years ago, when trying to convince a buyer at the local Mercedes Benz dealer to buy my higher-priced paper. The buyer said, "Well, yes, your paper does look better, but the other paper works well and it's cheaper." "I'm surprised to hear you say that." "Why?" the buyer asked. I paused and said, "After all, you are Mercedes Benz." The buyer at Mercedes Benz bought the paper. Are customers or clients walking like their company talks? If not, a gentle reminder might help.

■ *Get back to the customer, if necessary.* Drawbacks are not always black-and-white issues, and you may not always be able to resolve them on the spot. Whenever you feel that you can't honestly tell the customer whether or not you can satisfy a certain need, be truthful. Say that you'll have to check with others in your organization before you can provide an accurate response, or refer the customer to those people directly.

> Salespeople should know how to sell things by putting themselves in the customer's shoes.

■ *Be willing to walk away from the sale.* Your objective in resolving drawbacks should never be to pull the wool over the customer's eyes or to fool the customer. That tactic will always backfire, once the customer realizes the deficiency in your product or service. If you can't satisfy a customer's critical need, say so—even if it means you won't do business together. In the long run, it's better to sacrifice an immediate sale if it means protecting your credibility and that of your organization.

> Top salespeople are honest about their product. They admit what it can't do as well as what it can do.

CONVERT THE SKEPTIC

Alligator Trap
Hesitant Customers Just Need to See More Teeth

Alligators have no time to reassure their customers. They figure that after enough talking, the customer will simply give in. But when a good salesperson senses hesitation, he or she must take such feelings seriously.

Every salesperson has to deal with skeptical customers. There may be times when you make a presentation, for example, and the customer will respond by saying, "You haven't convinced me," "They all make that claim," or "I'm sorry, but I just don't believe you."

Though skepticism is a negative buying attitude, it usually indicates real interest on the part of the customer. Studies

> When the customer doubts my product's ability to perform, I tell the customer to call a reference or I invite the customer to a demonstration.

have shown that when customers express skepticism, they're often looking for reassurance that your product or service will do what you say it will do—and they want to hear more from you.

Whenever you encounter skepticism, probe to discover the real concern behind the doubt and then offer appropriate proofs. Let the customer guide you in deciding what kind of proof will be most convincing, and always confirm that the customer's doubts have been removed. Another salesperson reports:

> Try as I may, I could not overcome my prospective customer's skepticism. Finally, a lightbulb went on. One of my most satisfied customers had been initially skeptical about my solutions to similar issues. I asked her to speak to the prospect. She was so compelling that they were convinced and we got the business.

DEMONSTRATE YOUR INTEGRITY

Some customers adopt a skeptical posture with every salesperson. They may even take pride in making things difficult. Several factors account for this mind-set:

- *The belief that salespeople can't be trusted.* Some people believe that all salespeople are basically unethical and that they'll do whatever they can to make a sale.
- *The need to establish their authority.* Some people believe that if they establish themselves as a force to be reckoned with, the salesperson won't take advantage of them.
- *The desire to make the best possible deal.* Some people believe that by questioning everything the salesperson says, they're more likely to win concessions and cut a good deal.

Much of this thinking stems from archaic images of the salesperson or prejudices against the sales profession. It assumes a win-lose relationship between the salesperson and the customer, a relationship that is inherently antagonistic.

Demonstrating your professionalism and integrity right from the start is the best way to counteract this kind of thinking. By showing that you want to help the customer and by focusing on meeting real customer needs, you establish yourself as a trusted resource for the customer instead of an adversary or a nuisance.

VERIFY THE DOUBT

In most cases, skepticism is an expression of real concern, a doubt the customer has about a specific feature or benefit of your product or service. Sometimes the customer expresses this skepticism directly and verbally, with phrases such as:

> Top salespeople have instant credibility. Associating with them rubs off on you. They have a direct way of getting down to business, a direct way of looking at you and making contact.

"Are you sure about that?"

"How can I really believe you?"

"I've heard that one before."

"I just don't buy what you're saying."

Sometimes the customer expresses this skepticism indirectly through:

- *Facial expressions*—narrowed or rolled eyes, a wrinkled forehead.
- *Body language*—arms and legs crossed, body tilted backward.
- *Voice quality*—a questioning or high-pitched tone.

> Recognizing body language and reading people are key selling skills.

Whenever the customer expresses skepticism directly or even *appears* skeptical, ask why. Say, "You don't look totally convinced to me. Is there anything I've said that bothers or confuses you?" Probe to isolate the source of the skepticism and determine its importance to the customer. That will help you to choose an appropriate form of proof to overcome the skepticism.

PROVIDE PROOFS

When presenting proofs that show you can do what you promise, always make sure they relate directly to the area of doubt, the specific feature or benefit that the customer is skeptical about.

There are many types and degrees of proof that you can present: letters from satisfied customers, photos, or published articles. These may or may not satisfy the skeptical customer. Testimonials from longtime customers that cite specific results are a better proof than a general, laudatory letter. And you can't go wrong with a long list of customers who are willing to talk to the skeptic. You might say, "If you'd like to speak to other businesspeople who are currently using our product, here are the names and numbers of some managers who'd be happy to talk to you."

You might even consider having the customer use your product or service on a trial basis—or offer a money-back guarantee. In any case, be sure to agree with the customer, in advance, on what would be satisfactory evidence. When you need to prove your claim, clarify what information they will need and provide documentation. Check with a technical person and then check back with the customer.

More Tips

■ *Document successful sales.* Today's customers are more knowledgeable and more demanding than ever—and more likely to question everything you say. That's why it's a good idea to develop a database of proofs—evidence you can readily draw from whenever you encounter skepticism during a sale. Include reports on the successful results you've achieved with previous or established customers, and make sure those accounts are well documented and up-to-date.

■ *Ask for customer endorsements.* No matter how much printed evidence you can offer, you're much more likely to dispel a customer's doubts by having him or her hear from one of your established, satisfied customers. Whenever you feel you've made a sale that's really helped a customer, ask for a written endorsement that spells out clearly what the customer achieved. Even better:

> The level of competence demanded of salespeople will take quantum leaps in the near future. They'll need to be more professional because customers are becoming more sophisticated.

Ask the customer for permission to add his or her name and phone number to a list of satisfied customers that you routinely provide to prospects.

■ *Mobilize third-party support.* Customers are always more willing to believe what you say when you can provide confirmation from reputable and disinterested third parties, such as a trade association or a business watchdog group. Equally effective is to encourage

> Top salespeople back up selected knowledge with references and evidence that their product is better than the competition's.

a trade journal to test or review your product or service, and include a copy of what they say in your packet of product literature.

■ *Establish a catalog of common doubts.* When you sell the same product or service over a long period of time, you'll probably notice that customers tend to express skepticism at similar points in the selling cycle or about the same features and benefits. Therefore, to prepare more effectively for your sales calls, you might want to develop a list of the most common doubts customers express and what proofs best counteract them. Be sure to add to your catalog whenever new proofs are developed.

SECTION FOUR

PARTNERING FOR THE LONG TERM

I used to sell computers; now I sell securities. No matter what I'm selling, my ears get tired hearing customers declare, "What's important to me is how will your goods and services continue to help me in the future?" As for me, what's important is repeat business; that's easier than moving my tail end up the swampland.

One thing you need to do keep the business is to watch out for poachers because they will invade your territory and steal your customers. Don't get caught bellied up as I once did.

I was selling my services to this old bullfrog. I told him I would keep his corner of the marsh safe from competitors and predators. In fact, working with me could help him capture a greater share of the marsh. I emphasized that I would be there for him through many saw grass seasons. Using the customer's lingo, I let him know that I was not a tadpole when it came to knowing his insect business.

He signed with me; but opted out of the renewal. Some lowlife lizard firm charmed him away! He said my actions didn't

In the relationships business, you can't be shortsighted. You must identify and constantly keep in mind the customer's short- and long-term goals. A total customer focus requires a sales representative to be flexible, creative, adaptable, patient, and knowledgeable about the customer's business, needs, and the industry environment.

match what came out of my mouth. He was wrong; my mouth is always where the action is!

Alligators may rely on their verbal ability to retain their clientele, but good salespeople need to use a variety of techniques. That's the only way to gain loyal customers whom you can count on to sustain your business and to help it grow. As more competitors crowd the marketplace and customer expectations rise, loyalty becomes ever more difficult to achieve and, once gained, can be quickly lost.

Customer partnerships don't come easily and they don't happen overnight. Start now to partner with your customers for the long term. Begin to establish the trust that partnerships require and to demonstrate the qualities that customers look for most in their partners: integrity, reliability, and a quality product or service. A client we know said: "If I buy only once, it is the product that interests me. But if I want to establish a good business relationship over a long period of time, then I look for a supplier who demonstrates integrity."

Make the effort to become the kind of sales professional with whom today's customers want to partner by keeping your commitments, focusing on your customer's needs, and showing that you're consistently dependable. Prove that you can be a valuable business consultant as well as a long-term friend and ally, and demonstrate your skills in mobilizing your own company's resources on behalf of the customer.

Persistence and a working-smart approach are essential to achieving customer loyalty, but the process of building partnerships with customers also requires considerable sensitivity. The best customer-supplier relationships are characterized by:

- *Close rapport*—You have a mutual understanding. You know what your goals are and how you like to work together.
- *Easy communication*—You communicate frequently and honestly and don't hesitate to confront problems. Long-standing partnerships have a more informal relationship and easier communication. You can say what you mean.
- *A personal dimension*—You enjoy working together and you care about each other's success.

> The salesperson embodies the integrity of the company by keeping promises, being honest, and acknowledging mistakes.

Treat your customer as a true partner by establishing a relationship of equality, based on honesty, mutual respect, and the desire to achieve common goals. When invited, participate in the customer's decision-making processes and work *for* the customer. Find the most appropriate solutions to the customer's problems, and then identify which of those solutions you can provide.

> The best salespeople are treated like employees of their customers. They may even have an office at the customer's plant.

The advantages of creating partnerships with customers are obvious. If you're currently selling, you know that retaining a customer is usually more profitable than trying to recruit a new one. But the key word here is "profitable." No one wants to maintain a relationship that's not rewarding, and some long-term customers require so much time—and demand so many concessions—that their business isn't worth the investment you make in them.

It therefore becomes imperative to develop a strategy for building profitable customer partnerships. First, define all those factors that contribute to excellence in sales performance and that help differentiate your company: superior selling and negotiation skills, efficient sales force automation, and effective team selling. Then develop measures to track those factors and ensure their continuous improvement.

> Top salespeople have the ability to walk away from customers if the partnership doesn't suit their company's business plan. They know how to say no diplomatically and can keep a relationship without turning people off.

For continuous process improvement, you have to have a model in place along with all the measures and tools to know how you are performing at any given moment. Then you have to keep pushing the model to get more productivity out of it, to get higher quality from the sales process, and to get more customer satisfaction at the other end.

Integrate customer assessments into your sales strategy. Segment your customers like many organizations segment their market. Work hard to win the loyalty of the "right" customers, but work just as earnestly to weed out the "wrong" ones. Ask yourself which customers are the most profitable? Which have the greatest potential? Which are likely to increase our revenues *and* our profits? Keep in mind that partnering with every customer is neither possible nor desirable.

> Salespeople need the typical traits, such as working hard and a high energy level, but the vision—the ability to see the customer's unique requirements and the best fit—is what separates the best performers.

Once you've identified a customer worth partnering with, then do everything you can to link your products or services to the business objectives of the customer's organization. An in-depth knowledge of the customer's operational strategies, culture, and business processes will help you to develop innovative, customized solutions that fit into the customer's long-term plans.

Also, work through your primary contact to pursue relationships at different levels within the customer's organization. That will that help you to achieve greater penetration into the account (and improve your profitability). It will also provide contact with other important decision makers, allow you to better understand the customer's multiple objectives, and put you in a better position to address the customer's total requirements.

Above all, never become complacent. Don't confuse customer satisfaction with customer loyalty. Just because your customers are satisfied now doesn't mean that they'll stay with you, especially when the competition offers an incentive for them to switch.

Seek out the training and coaching that you'll need to constantly improve your selling skills and achieve better results. Work with your manager at refining your sales strategy and the process you use to build customer relationships. Never stop trying to understand your customers better. Think of yourself (or your organization) as a consumer and routinely ask yourself: Who are we satisfied with? To whom are we loyal? What really accounts for the difference?

USE A CONSULTATIVE SELLING APPROACH

Alligator Trap
Dominate the Relationship

When alligators deal with prospects, they think predominantly in the short term, taking the what-can-you-do-for-me-now approach. Good salespeople must remember to think long term if they want to stay afloat in today's competitive environment.

A salesperson can no longer survive in today's marketplace simply by making a quick "pitch" or by staging a flashy presentation of your product or service. These days, a salesperson must gain an in-depth knowledge of the customer's goals and work collaboratively with the customer to achieve them—that is, to become a consultative salesperson.

As a consultative salesperson, you must interact with the customer in new ways: as a close ally, a trusted advisor, and a business resource. You have to be consultative, you have to understand the customer's business and ask questions about what's relevant, and you have to show that you know what's going on in the buyer's industry.

The salesperson is the orchestra leader who trys to keep all sections playing together at the same time. The percussion, woodwinds, strings, and brass sections of an orchestra can't do their own thing in their own time. It is the same in the sales cycle. All components of the sales organization and the customer's organization must work in sync.

Using this selling approach transforms the sales call from a one-sided conversation into a highly interactive dialogue between partners. It promotes the free and open exchange of information, so that the customer and you can identify critical needs and work together to create unique, effective solutions that meet those needs.

To become a consultative salesperson, you must demonstrate the qualities that customers look for in a business partner:

- *Commitment*—Your overriding goal is to help the customer achieve his or her long-term business objectives.
- *Involvement*—You call frequently and remain close to the customer even when there's no prospect of an immediate sale.
- *Strategic focus*—You deliver creative, customized solutions to the customer's needs.

Studies of top salespeople reveal three roles that describe consultative salespeople: business consultant, long-term ally, and strategic orchestrator. These roles represent critical dimensions that turn the flat, cartoonlike sales character into a three-dimensional effective salesperson.

ACT AS A BUSINESS CONSULTANT

As a business consultant, you must educate customers about products and services in the context of the customer's "big picture." As mentioned earlier, this requires a thorough knowledge of the customer's business and marketplace, a keen awareness of the customer's competition, and an accurate assessment of what the customer needs to gain market share.

Critical to the role of business consultant is your ability to demonstrate integrity and contribute solid insights into the customer's business challenges. When you offer the customer valuable guidance and advice, you transcend the traditional roles of vendor and supplier and enter into a new, closer, and potentially more beneficial relationship with the customer.

Three factors are especially important in establishing yourself as a business consultant:

- *Your knowledge.* Today's customers don't have time to educate you about their company or industry. You must acquire a deep understanding of the

Clients and customers have dramatically changed their buying habits. Salespeople have to adapt to this new situation; they must become advisors. They must offer clients a full package of advice and service.

Customers want to work with salespeople who are aware of the fast-moving business environment and are able to offer up-to-date advice.

customer's business challenges and bottom-line realities, and arm yourself with useful information that can benefit the customer.

- *Your communication skills.* Expressing yourself clearly and persuasively is essential to becoming an effective business consultant. Equally important, however, is your ability to listen actively, demonstrate understanding, and probe effectively.

- *Your attitude.* Positive thinking and enthusiasm aren't the only personal qualities salespeople need today. To succeed as a business consultant, you also must be sensitive to the customer's feelings, perceptive of the situation surrounding the customer, and flexible to accommodate the customer's wishes.

BECOME A LONG-TERM ALLY

In the role of long-term ally, you must work closely with the customer, even when there's no immediate sale involved. This requires that you maintain regular contact with the customer, demonstrate concern for the customer's interests, and develop a track record of providing value to the customer.

Critical to the role of long-term ally is your ability to establish trust, nurture the bond between your organization and the customer's, and strengthen the quality of the business relationship. When you work to build an alliance with the customer, you transcend the limitations of transaction selling and focus on managing the relationship over the long term, not just during the sale.

Three actions help you establish yourself as a long-term ally:

- *Create a positive image of your organization.* Demonstrate the credibility of your organization by positioning your product or service realistically, and by making honest comparisons with the offerings of your competitors. Be willing to turn down business that's not in the customer's long-term interests.

■ *Solicit feedback from the customer.* Demonstrate your concern by continually asking questions that establish the customer's level of satisfaction with your product or service and with the solutions you offer. Ask what you can do to help the customer do his or her job better.

■ *Add value through the relationship.* Work effectively with the customer to meet the customer's needs, solve the customer's problems, and help the customer's business to grow. Focus on your customer's customers, and determine what you can do to increase their satisfaction.

> Customers expect you to educate them on how they are doing and how they could do it better.

PLAY THE ROLE OF STRATEGIC ORCHESTRATOR

In the role of strategic orchestrator, you must marshal all your company's resources to effectively meet the customer's needs. This may involve recruiting colleagues to solve production, delivery, or service problems, or it may involve interacting with the customer as the head of a sales team.

Critical to this role is your ability to maintain good relationships within your own company and coordinate all the information, resources, and activities needed to support the customer before, during, and after the sale. This allows you to provide a total organizational response to the customer's needs and to deliver completely on the promises that you make.

These competencies help you to establish yourself as a strategic orchestrator:

> **Customers expect salespeople to coordinate their company's resources according to customer requirements.**

■ *Knowledge of your company's structure.* Know the various functions within your company and the responsibilities and talents of colleagues within those functions. Ask yourself, How can they help to add value for the customer?

■ *Expertise in building and managing a team.* Maintain good working relationships at all levels of your organization—with superiors, colleagues, and support staff. Use your influence, communication skills, and powers of persuasion to build a team that's able to meet the customer's needs.

■ *Ability to coordinate delivery and service to customers.* Coordinate all aspects of product and service delivery, and make sure the customer knows what's happening at every step in the process. A client we know said that one salesperson mobilized his sales organization and eventually solved the problem in such a way that it left him feeling that he could do business with this guy. Determine if any additional resources are needed to serve the customer properly—and then go out and get them.

■ *Ability to manage priorities and performance.* Establish realistic but challenging performance goals, and achieve them by setting specific, short-term objectives. Monitor progress, identify setbacks and bottlenecks, and develop action plans to remedy performance problems.

More Tips

■ *Beef up your business expertise.* Your effectiveness in playing the role of business consultant depends to a large extent on the knowledge you demonstrate of your customers' companies, of the industries you sell to, and of the marketplace in general. So, work constantly to build up your body of knowledge. Identify any significant gaps in your understanding of business issues and develop an action plan to close them. Read business journals and trade publications, seek customers' and colleagues' perceptions of market trends, and use your contacts to acquire information about a customer's company.

- *Create a database of customer knowledge.* A good way to improve your knowledge of current and prospective customers is to compile a comprehensive database that you can research whenever the need arises. Set the database up as a team project for your department and ask for input from co-workers and managers. Include annual reports of your customer's companies, articles from newspapers and magazines, even product brochures.

- *Increase your visibility.* You can solidify relationships with customers by maintaining frequent and regular contact. After a purchase, reorder, or implementation, call to check things out. Set up monthly or bimonthly meetings to review ongoing issues or problems. Invite the customer to business lectures or to presentations you give at industry conferences. Whatever you do, make sure the customer knows that you're interested in how well he or she is doing and that you value the relationship.

- *Eliminate the "relationship gap."* In transaction selling, the salesperson's level of interest is typically highest before and during the sale; it then drops off substantially once the sale is made. The customer's level of interest, however, follows a different pattern; it doesn't peak until later, when the customer is concerned about the successful implementation of the product and how well it will work. To establish yourself as a long-term ally of your customers, you must eliminate this "relationship gap." How? By demonstrating your commitment over the long term and by ensuring consistent service and support to the customer at every step in the sales process. Don't let it be said about you what one customer said about a salesperson: "I cannot trust a supplier who tries to take advantage of me or my company. If that happens, I break off the relationship right away."

■ *Manage your accounts, don't just sell to them.* The best salespeople see themselves as stewards of the customer-supplier relationship, and serve as the primary contact between the two organizations. Instead of focusing only on making a sale, they assume responsibility for monitoring every aspect of the relationship and keep in touch with all the people in their organization—in production, warehouse, shipping dock, or billing department—who serve the customer.

A banker once said:

> At my bank, part of our business is helping people achieve the great American dream. We're in it for the long term; a customer is a customer for life. It's pure relationship selling.

14 LESSON

WORK EASILY WITH TEAMS

Alligator Trap
Don't Trust Others to Look Out for Your Interests

Alligators prefer to work solo. They can keep more for themselves that way. But good salespeople operate with a different mentality. They understand the greater rewards that come from using a team approach.

Teams are everywhere! Whether you sell to large corporations, small businesses, or family-owned companies, chances are you've sold to a buying team. That's because customer requirements are more complicated these days, so many customers are setting up teams to explain what they need from suppliers and to evaluate what suppliers can offer.

Selling teams have also become common. Leading suppliers now recognize that it's unrealistic to have only a single point of contact between the customer and the sales organization. To sell more effectively, many now utilize selling teams, which are groups of experts who demonstrate a comprehensive knowledge of the customer's business and industry and who can work together to meet the customer's total requirements.

Team selling differentiates you from your competitors by allowing you to provide a wide range of information, advice, and ideas to your customers. It may also help you to respond better when:

> Total customer focus is a corporate mindset that is critical in today's market. It's important to manage others—your colleagues in sales and other staff throughout your organization—to work in concert with you.

- You're dealing with multiple contacts in a large account.
- You must satisfy a customer who has complex needs or especially high expectations.
- The sale involves highly technical issues, extensive sales support, or a complicated implementation.

Being part of a selling team enables you to advance the sale by demonstrating the power of your organization, and it confirms that your entire organization is behind the sale. What's more, by teaming up with other experts from your company, you can respond better to questions that surface during sales discussions. You avoid having to say to the customer: "I'm sorry, but I can't answer that question. Is it OK if I get back to you?"

ANALYZE THE BUYING TEAM

When you're dealing with a buying team, you know that you often must satisfy everyone on that team. If possible, learn what role each member of the buying team plays to help guide your efforts and ensure that each player receives the proper attention.

When analyzing a buying team, you should consider:

- *The size of the team.* When the buying team includes only two or three members, you may be able to handle the sale yourself. If four or more members are involved, however, you may require support from others in your company or you might have to overcome a number of hurdles before making the sale.

- *The functions or departments represented.* The functional profile of the team will give you an idea of the customer's priorities and concerns. For example, if the finance department is heavily represented, expect either pricing or payment terms to be a major issue.

- *The titles of team members.* If the customer stacks the team with high-ranking managers, you may want to invite your own manager to participate in your presentation or ask executives from your company who hold comparable titles to come along.

- *The key decision makers.* Every buying team includes members who carry more weight than others in the buying decision. Find out who these key decision makers are and focus your efforts on meeting their needs.

Team selling is the only way to go as you move from single products into more sophisticated systems. Technical support people, administrative support people, and installation people all must work together to meet the customer's requirements.

Decision making used to be done by just one department; now everyone is involved.

DEVELOP A TEAM STRATEGY

When you need to form a team to support your sales effort, it's vital that you identify the roles and responsibilities for each member of your team. Try to match customer requirements closely with individual experts from your company, but don't involve too many players in the sales process— only those who are best prepared to answer the customer's questions or concerns.

Decide on an objective for the call to help you decide which resources are required. Then develop a sales call strategy for your team: What is your plan for who will do what, say what, and when? Take into account different personalities, communication styles, and expertise. One person might be able to deal effectively with certain aspects of the call or certain customer attitudes while another person might deal more effectively with other aspects.

Also decide how team members will participate in the call: in person, over the phone, or by video teleconferencing. It's usually more effective when the entire team shows up to face the customer, but this may not always be possible if team members work in different locations or divisions.

Designate a team leader for the sales call. It doesn't have to be you. You can introduce a technical expert who takes the lead while you play the role of facilitator, ensuring that the call stays on track. Or you can be the primary spokesperson and call on various members of your team as the need arises. The head of one organization says that the best salespeople are team captains, not individual stars. A resource-intensive sale requires leaders who want to manage all team members.

After the sales call, always conduct a debriefing session with your team to share observations and ideas, and decide whose participation will be needed for future calls.

BUILD UP YOUR SALES TEAM

To ensure team success, train team members in the appropriate selling, communication, and teamwork skills. Fully educate team members on the background of the customer, the current sales situation, and on the objectives of the sales call. Then conduct a dry run to make sure everyone understands his or her part in the call, how to respond to customer queries tactfully and comprehensively, and what kind of information may have to be collected or prepared beforehand. Everyone—from sales, administration, service— has to work together effectively as a team. All should be taught interpersonal communication skills, so that they can work together more effectively to meet the customer's needs.

In the future, salespeople will have to develop leadership skills and be able to practice them at every level. They will have to be able to motivate others.

Finally, keep team members informed of the status of the sale between calls. Because you're the primary customer contact, it's your responsibility to coordinate communication between the customer and the sales team and to let team members know how the customer is receiving their efforts.

More Tips

- *Describe the team process to the customer.* Whenever you decide to use a selling team with one of your customers, always inform that customer before the call, explain how the process will work, and name the people you'll be bringing along. Not only does this prepare the customer for the call, but also it boosts your credibility by making the customer aware of the wide network of resources that stand behind you and of the added value that you can bring to the sale.

> In the future, salespeople will work on multifunctional teams. The salesperson must have a strong feel for team spirit. There won't be any more "Lone Rangers."

■ *Reward team members.* Unless team members are compensated in some way for their contribution, they may be reluctant to devote their time and effort to helping you sell. Though it may not be necessary to share your commission from the sale, do whatever you can to make it worthwhile for team members to participate; for example, establish a bonus pool, share credit for the sale, or celebrate the close of the sale by taking team members and their spouses to a fancy restaurant.

■ *Promote the benefits of team selling.* If you feel that team selling is the best way to meet your customers' needs, then do whatever you can to promote its value and to integrate it into your culture. Identify and address factors that may inhibit the success of team selling in your organization (e.g., departmental barriers, inefficient communication channels) and ask for the training and coaching that's needed to make team selling work.

■ *Develop team spirit.* One of the most formidable challenges of team selling is getting salespeople to share responsibility for the sale and to collaborate with others. You may be used to selling alone, but remember that the success of your team depends strongly on your ability to work together with others and demonstrate team spirit. Patience, flexibility, and consideration are critical qualities for salespeople in a team selling environment.

ESTABLISH MULTIPLE RELATIONSHIPS

Alligator Trap
Focus Only on Your Next Meal

Alligators don't really take the time with prospects to meet others in the same family. Their contacts are usually limited and brief! It takes a good salesperson to know that every relationship can be the stepping-stone to a much broader client base. Expert salespeople consistently pursue a relationship with the entire customer organization. They establish multiple relationships in *each* of their accounts.

It's often more efficient to sell to new buying centers in an established account than to break into a new company. After all, you already know the goals and strategies of the organization, you have built-in credibility, and—because the buying centers might all be in the same location—you save time prospecting and presenting. Achieving greater penetration in an existing account almost always proves to be profitable.

Top salespeople also recognize the importance of establishing multiple relationships when their primary contact moves on. Knowing other buyers in key areas of an account, including possible replacements for the decision maker who's no longer around, offers you protection for the future.

DEVELOP CONTACTS AT ALL LEVELS

In order to partner effectively with the customer and to have an in-depth understanding of the customer's needs, you should work to establish relationships at a variety of levels within the customer's organization. Not only will this expose you to different aspects of the business and help you to develop a broader perspective on the customer, but also it will allow you to expand your customer base.

> It's easy to get to know one person within an organization, but you'll experience greater success in penetrating new departments and establishing relationships at higher levels and in multiple buying centers.

If possible, start by talking to those at your contact's level who head other departments or functions; then talk to their direct reports. This will give you an understanding of the organization's strategic objectives as well as its production, tactical, and front-line challenges. Once you have gained that understanding, it will make it easier for you to approach and sell to those at a high level within an organization. Ideally, you should leverage your relationships for maximum penetration, so there are always a number of people in the organization whom you can call.

TARGET TOP DECISION MAKERS

Find the customer behind the customer and try to make contacts as high up as possible, even if they don't have the need to buy from you. By focusing your relationship-building efforts on top decision makers, you'll gain solid support in the organization and increase your visibility.

The best way to penetrate an account is to ask your initial contact if he or she knows other people in the company who might need your services. You can then approach those people on your own or, better, ask your contact to introduce you to them. Having your initial contact at your side acts as an endorsement, and it sends a positive message about you to other potential buyers in the organization.

Try to identify the decision-making styles and improvement goals of each player with whom you come in contact. For example, ask about the process they used to make previous purchases and how well those purchases helped them achieve their business objectives. Though you may not be able to apply this information immediately, it could prove helpful in future

> Top salespeople take the time to know the customer overall—beyond knowing only the people who make purchasing decisions—from both an analytical and personal point of view.

sales opportunities within the organization. You wear many hats in a sales account. You serve different needs for each person you meet with; for example, you need to be an analyst for the president. You need to be a motivator and a deal maker for agents.

Be careful not to go over someone's head to make a sale, particularly if your original contact is the one who's responsible for evaluating you. And never slight a contact at a lower level just to get to a higher-up. The day may come when that higher-ranking contact moves on, and your original contact is the only person left in the organization who still knows you.

More Tips

■ *Avoid the "hit and run" sales approach.* Some salespeople are so eager to make their next sale that they move too quickly to new prospects and neglect potential buyers within an existing account. Establishing multiple relationships means you understand the customer's organizational structure and investigate all sales opportunities within the account. Ask yourself, What other departments or functions have needs that are similar to those of my current buyer? Are there other divisions that have departments similar to the one I'm selling to now?

> Salespeople must develop a broader knowledge of various subjects. Today, they are good discussion partners on an operational level. In the future, they ought to communicate on a higher level.

■ *Polish your face-to-face selling skills.* Though it's possible to make new contacts within an existing account simply by making phone calls, you'll be more successful by doing it face-to-face. People take you more seriously when you're physically present—not just a disembodied voice at the end of a telephone—and will usually give you more of their time and attention. What's more, it boosts your credibility if you can walk into someone's office and say, "I just had a meeting with Sue Thompson down the hall, and she thought it would be a good idea if I stopped in and introduced myself to you."

■ *Adjust your communication style.* Your ability to deal effectively with people at a variety of levels depends, at least in part, on how comprehensive your knowledge is of their organization. With middle-management contacts, you must be able to demonstrate a strong understanding of technical and implementation problems. With executive-level contacts, you must be able to focus on strategic considerations and discuss high-level business issues.

16

LESSON

MAINTAIN A COMPETITIVE ADVANTAGE

Alligator Trap
The Competition's Scarce When You Rule the Swamp

Alligators often turn a blind eye to their competitors. When it comes to worrying about how a rival might be doing, they can't see past their noses! But good salespeople know that many factors contribute to the buying decision, and that in today's business environment the key to winning customers—and gaining their loyalty—is being able to differentiate yourself from your competition.

Each of your customers faces a unique combination of strategic needs and business issues. When you offer your customers more than your competitors, the less likely your customers will take their business elsewhere. To maintain this competitive edge, however, you can never become complacent. You must continually come up with more creative solutions to customer problems, provide more

The building blocks in the sales process are critical to success: how salespeople present themselves, how they meet the customer's needs and goals, and how collateral materials are presented. Make sure your recommendations are creative and customized. You want the customer to recognize your integrity, understanding, creativity, and commitment to their goals.

value-added services, and identify new opportunities to help the customer.

As the products and services of competitors become more similar, you help differentiate yourself through the value that *you* bring to the customer relationship: by demonstrating your professionalism as a salesperson, by applying your intelligence to solving problems, and by establishing yourself as a business resource customers can depend on.

IDENTIFY BUYING CRITERIA

When you accurately identify the criteria your customers use to buy, you may be able to position your product or service more favorably than your competitors.

This isn't always easy to do because customer expectations are constantly changing—and rising. In the past, most customers were satisfied with a quality product at a fair price. These days customer do much more scrutinizing of buying decisions. Management expects its buyers to do it all, at lower cost. They often demand much more: after-sale support, electronic data interface, or specially designed solutions.

Never make assumptions about the criteria your customer uses to evaluate suppliers. Research the customer's business extensively, identify the customer's short- and long-term needs, and get to know the people who are making the buying decision.

Analyze your customer's buying criteria by asking:

- *How is the customer changing?* Is the customer entering new markets? Has the customer's strategy changed? What new business goals is the customer trying to meet?

- *How is the market changing?* How well is the customer doing in the current business environment? What trends affect the customer? How are the customer's customers changing?

- *Who will make the buying decision?* Why were certain people selected to make the buying decision? What are the priorities of these decision makers? What criteria did they use in making previous buying decisions?

SIZE UP THE COMPETITION

Focus on keeping your competitive edge by studying your competition and by learning about

> Today's salespeople must bring their clients a full advice and service package.

> The customer's customer is driving him or her to become more competitive. Customers today have to make decisions based on criteria they previously would not have considered.

> Customers are buying both a concept and a product. They are looking for value for their money—and someone to make their business more profitable.

their strengths and weaknesses. Customers don't want to work with salespeople who know only their own products. Salespeople also must be familiar with the products and services offered by competitors. Make sure your company provides you with up-to-date competitive information: brochures, product samples, data on benefits, specs, prices, and delivery.

> **Knowing the competition's strengths and weaknesses—and your own strengths and weaknesses—gives you credibility.**

If you aren't sure who else is vying for the customer's business, ask the customer directly. Find out what suppliers the customer has used in the past. Why did the customer drop these suppliers? What was the customer looking for that they couldn't provide?

Then evaluate the customer's current suppliers. How long has the customer been working with them? Is the customer satisfied? If not, why not? What else does the customer want that these suppliers can't provide?

Be able to articulate the differences between your product or service and that of your competitors. Emphasize your exclusive benefits: those elements or services that only you, not your competitors, can provide. Identify the areas where you excel by asking:

- Can we provide the same benefits to the customer at a lower price?
- Can we offer the customer higher quality, better service, and faster delivery?
- Can we make performance guarantees that the competition can't?
- Can we meet the customer's needs more completely or more efficiently?

A salesperson we know told us the following story, which illustrates how knowing your competition gives you the competitive edge.

> She agreed that we could save her money and that we had met all the criteria needed to do business with her. But she still wouldn't change. It wasn't that important to her and it was too much trouble, especially if we "messed up" the work of the current vendor, who was not doing anything wrong.
>
> We knew our competition was an aggressive smaller company with excellent service, good pricing, and strong representation. Its drawbacks were weak computer systems and reporting, and limited program and product-line offerings. We also knew this prospective account was a company that had been sold several years ago and was again on the selling block.
>
> I asked her, "You mentioned your company was up for sale again. Did you go through a lot of changes during the last sale?" Of course they did and she expressed the trauma. I went on to demonstrate how our system would meet the need if new owners wanted to see detailed results by department, and I stressed other capabilities the current vendor did not have. She finally agreed to give us a trial period!

> To sell something, you have to be able to sell yourself first and your company second. When products and services are virtually identical, the difference lies in the salesperson.

SHOWCASE YOURSELF

Consider your role in the sales equation. Ask yourself, What can *I* offer the customer that competing salespeople can't? Remember, the extra value you bring to a customer relationship stems directly from you; for example, your wide-ranging expertise as a business consultant, unique skills at managing the sales process, or previous experience at solving customer problems.

Emphasize all the additional roles you can play that will add value to the relationship, including:

- *Information specialist.* Can you provide articles, white papers, or research results that will interest the customer?

- *Resource manager.* Are you familiar with experts, consultants, or researchers who can help the customer?

- *Technical advisor.* Do you have any specialized technical training that might benefit the customer?

- *Decision advisor.* Do you have the experience and skills to help the customer make sound business decisions?

Salespeople must be decision advisors, because their clients have evolved into decision makers. Salespeople who aren't decision advisors are out of touch with customers, unable to understand customers or to respond to their needs.

GAIN A HIGH-TECH ADVANTAGE

The creative use of advanced information technologies also can give you a competitive edge today. Not only do computers allow you to streamline the sales process by automating certain steps, but they also can help you to improve the quality of your performance—and facilitate decision making—when you're with your customers. For example, putting an office in a briefcase—phone, E-mail, computer, fax, CD-ROM—allows salespeople to immediately access all kinds of information during a sales call, including technical data, the status of a delivery, new developments in the customer's company or industry, or other information on topics of interest to the customer.

You also can use a laptop computer to quickly customize a solution and show it to a customer on the spot; for example, providing details on price and delivery, comparisons with competitors' offerings, and projections of its bottom-line impact.

ESTABLISH BEST PRACTICES

Top sales organizations identify what works best with customers and they constantly improve those tactics and practices, whether it's team selling, consultative selling, or sales force automation. This gives salespeople a competitive edge, because they develop more productive and efficient sales calls and avoid wasting time on misdirected efforts.

You can improve the quality of your selling by examining your sales practices from the customer's perspective. That involves getting feedback from customers either informally, in your conversations with them, or by measuring customer satisfaction systematically, through opinion surveys and focus groups. This feedback will help you to determine:

> Information systems allow the buyer and you to examine many options you might otherwise have overlooked. And companies should be well equipped with computer systems and software that help you analyze the situation. You cannot go to war without arms.

- The roles that customers want you to play.
- The competencies that customers look for in you.
- The high-value activities that customers expect from you.

Applying business process improvement techniques also can help you to reengineer your organization's sales process and make it more cost-effective. Here, your objective is to identify those high-leverage activities that are critical to productivity and customer satisfaction and that will help differentiate you from your competition. One sales organization always measures sales performance in terms of end results: quotas, growth, new accounts, and so forth. That may not be the best or only way to measure performance; it also needs to look at the steps of the process and manage those.

> Honesty is very important. Eventually, customers will spot a fake product.

Benchmarking with leading sales organizations also can help you to develop an effective model for selling and to define those "best practices" that should be replicated in your organization as standard selling procedures.

More Tips

- *Work to exceed customer expectations.* Chances are the product or service you sell is not unique to your industry; there are probably other suppliers who offer something similar to meet the customer's needs. To differentiate yourself in this situation, you have to provide *more* than what the customer needs and *exceed* his or her expectations. When you work to "delight" the customer (e.g., by offering just-in-time delivery or exceptional after-sale support), you can stand out from your competition, even when you're selling a commodity product.

- *Don't oversell the customer.* If you find yourself competing against a supplier who offers a product or service that's better than yours, don't try to make the sale by promising what you can't deliver. Today's savvy customers usually see through such tactics and won't want to deal with you again if they suspect you're overselling. A better approach: Yield gracefully to the competition. By showing that you're honest and that you have the customer's best interests in mind, you can sometimes score points and build the foundation for a future relationship with the customer.

■ *Excel at the basics.* Adding more bells and whistles to your product isn't the only way to differentiate yourself from your competition. When every player on the field is promising more discounts and add-ons, sometimes the best way to impress the customer is to show that you excel at the

> Top salespeople are brilliant at the basics.

basics: Establish your competence and credibility as a salesperson, demonstrate the quality of your product or service, and guarantee dependable after-sale support.

DON'T JUST NEGOTIATE— INNOVATE

Alligator Trap
With a Mouth Like Mine, There's No Need to Compromise

Alligators may negotiate initially, but ultimately they feel it's a waste of time. If a prospect can't accept an alligator's position, he or she will make a final decision that will end all negotiations permanently! Good salespeople can't afford to be so reptilian.

Successful negotiation is an art, one that requires patience and endurance, the ability to deal with conflict, and a willingness to take risks. The more skillfully you negotiate, the better your chances of reaching a mutually beneficial agreement with the customer and of closing the sale.

Almost anything can be negotiated, but careful planning and a cooperative atmosphere are essential, and concessions are part of the game. Whether you negotiate during the sales call or set up a special meeting to negotiate, remember that your objective is still to develop a long-term, profitable relationship with the customer.

> ## Salespeople have to be good at negotiating— negotiating a solution and negotiating a compromise when things aren't going as quickly or as well as they want.

Sometimes it's necessary to be creative, to "reengineer the opportunity" when no satisfactory solution appears for the customer's problem. This requires reviewing the situation with the customer to identify a new approach to the issues.

Suppose you sell laptop computers, but your customer expresses the desire to lease, not buy, your equipment for a limited period. You find out that the real issue behind this need is that the customer has to improve sales performance because the competition is gaining. You might now use this knowledge to leverage the sale; for example, emphasize the 24-hour on-line help you offer with every purchase agreement or explore working with another (noncompetitive) supplier to develop a totally customized laptop solution. You can form a new partnership with your customer by collaborating on an innovative solution geared toward a long-term commitment.

ESTABLISH AN AGENDA

Whenever there are differences between what you can offer the customer and what the customer needs, you may be able to overcome those differences by negotiating. Don't begin to negotiate until you get a conditional buying agreement from the customer. Then agree on the differences to be discussed and the order in which to discuss them. Usually it's best to begin with the difference that you think will be the easiest to resolve; this builds momentum and increases your motivation to work through more difficult issues.

Top salespeople understand the critical factors of the customer's business and put together the right solutions.

For each issue you negotiate, probe to reveal the customer's position. First, make sure you understand *which* customer needs are not being met and *why* they're important to the customer. Then make the customer aware of your needs. This helps the customer understand why it may be difficult or impossible for you to meet certain needs.

Customers will always test you to see what you will do for them.

BRAINSTORM ALTERNATIVES

To resolve your differences through negotiation, explore what-if scenarios with the customer to help you find alternatives that are acceptable to both you and the customer (e.g., changes in price or payment terms or new conditions of the sale).

Test the viability of each alternative by asking the customer hypothetical questions, such as:

- "What if we were to. . . ?"
- "Suppose we did things this way. . . ?"
- "Would it help you if we were to. . . ?"
- "How would you feel if we were to. . . ?"

Throughout your discussion, invite suggestions from the customer or allow the customer to bring in colleagues or co-workers who can contribute worthwhile ideas. You may also want to invite others from your company (e.g., salespeople you work with or your manager) who are good at brainstorming or have experience in conducting similar negotiations.

> Top salespeople are positive thinkers who continually try to offer more innovative and more distinctive solutions that bring more value to the customer. Top salespeople are more solution oriented than problem oriented.

Creativity and flexibility are the keys to successful negotiations. When brainstorming alternatives, keep your mind open and try to think of as many options as you can. The more ways that you or the customer can be flexible, the more likely you'll find workable alternatives that you both can live with.

When you run out of ideas or reach an impasse, don't panic. Sometimes all it takes is a short break or change of pace to help you get back on track. Suggest getting some coffee or lunch, for example, or leave the troublesome issue unresolved for the moment and move on to something new. You might even try a new problem-solving technique to recharge your creative juices. Top salespeople will possess a wide range of problem-solving strategies.

Don't commit to any alternative until the customer and you have explored all differences. The reason: Some alternatives may be mutually exclusive (e.g., you may agree to provide four technical advisors during an installation, but later negotiate a price that allows for only two). When an alternative proves acceptable to both of you, put it on hold until you can commit to a complete agreement.

KNOW WHEN TO CONCEDE

You can sometimes overcome differences with the customer by making concessions to the customer without getting anything in return. However, concessions must be used sparingly. If you concede too much, you can jeopardize the profitability of the sale or set an unfavorable precedent. The customer may then expect similar concessions in the future, and other customers may ask for the same concession.

Don't make *any* concessions until you know and understand *all* the customer's demands, and don't concede if it undermines your objectives. If you decide that you made a mistake after making a concession, don't be afraid to tell the customer and ask to reopen negotiations.

Two negotiation tactics can help you to avoid making concessions:

■ *Splitting the difference.* Find a mutually acceptable middle ground between your position and that of the customer. Example: The customer wants a 12-month warranty while you normally offer 6 months. You agree to split the difference and give the customer a 9-month warranty.

■ *Making a trade-off.* Give the customer something that he or she wants in return for something of comparable or greater value to you. Example: You offer the customer a 10 percent price cut in return for immediate payment in full.

More Tips

■ *Expect to negotiate.* When you negotiate in a prearranged meeting, you have time to

> The better the company understands the customer's needs—and is flexible enough and able enough to respond to them—the more successful it will be.

prepare for the negotiation beforehand by analyzing the situation and developing alternatives. But sometimes you have to negotiate on the spot, during a sales call. To make sure you're prepared for these spontaneous negotiations, always develop a negotiating plan along with your sales strategy; before you walk in, know what you can—and can't—give away. When you anticipate and plan for negotiations, you minimize your surprises and increase the probability of achieving a win-win agreement.

- *Confirm the customer's authority to negotiate.* Don't begin negotiating until you've established that your contact has the authority to alter the provisional purchase agreement. If your contact is not acting alone (e.g., he or she may be a member of a buying team), find out what other decision makers are involved in the sale and ask that they be brought into the discussions.

> A salesperson needs to combine strategy with the application of skills. Making your analysis before you call is critical. You can't just jump into the sale.

- *Prioritize customer needs.* Every customer has a variety of needs—some more important than others—and it helps your negotiation to know which ones have priority. If necessary, work with the customer to determine which needs *must* be satisfied and which are less urgent. This gives the customer greater latitude to negotiate and helps you to define areas where possible concessions or trade-offs can be made and identify issues that are definitely *not* negotiable.

- *Conduct internal negotiations.* On occasion, you might not be able to make concessions or trade-offs with the customer without gaining approval from your organization. In those situations, it's sometimes necessary to act as your customer's advocate and to conduct negotiations internally. To lay the foundation for successful internal negotiations, keep your manager informed of sales agreements as they develop, maintain healthy relationships with the people who will help you fulfill the final sales agreement, and stay on top of organizational changes that may affect the agreements you make. As one salesperson said, "When I'm at the client's, I represent my company. When I'm at my company, I represent the client."

Sometimes salespeople don't value their own or the customer's time. It's important to know when a sale isn't going to be made and to walk away.

■ *Know when to call it quits.* In any negotiation, you must establish a walkaway position— the point at which you're no longer willing to negotiate. When you're spending more time on the negotiation than the sale is worth, when the concessions the customer demands are too difficult to make, or when your profit margin on the sale becomes unacceptably low, be willing to call it quits. Do whatever you can to preserve the relationship, of course, but don't waste your time on a sale that doesn't benefit both the customer and you.

KEEP YOUR EYE ON THE FISH THAT GOT AWAY

Alligator Trap
Cut Your Losses and Focus on the Next Prospect

Alligators have been known to hide in the swamp for days when they don't get what they want. But good salespeople take a more realistic view of their losses.

Like every salesperson, you will lose customers—long-established customers as well as potential customers that you want and never land. Whether or not you close every sale, it's important to maintain your momentum and your motivation. You must focus your energies on gaining knowledge for the future and not dwell on disappointments or feelings of rejection.

Numerous factors may contribute to why a sale is won or lost. Find out all the details. Begin by reevaluating the initial viability of the prospect or the profitability of the account. Then develop a plan to collect information: Why didn't they buy? What factors account for the breakup? What can be done to win them in the future? What have you learned that can be applied to other customers and accounts?

Continue to maintain contact for the future by sending relevant articles or important information. Follow up on how well lost customers are continuing to have their needs met. If they went with a competitor, ask what more the customers wish the competitor could do. If the customers are getting by without your type of product or service, ask how well they're meeting their long-term objectives. Don't just call to "keep in touch"—contribute value in your follow-up conversations.

BE A GOOD LOSER

When a prospect decides to go with another supplier instead of you—or when an established customer drops you and hooks up with another organization—respect the customer's decision. A customer we know said when one salesperson lost out on a large deal, he took it very well, and the two continued after that on a professional basis. The salesman was a good loser and remained a professional. In many other experiences, the customer reported that salespeople were bad losers. Remember that customers have the right to choose the suppliers they want to work with, and can change their minds at will.

If you lose an account, never whine or complain to the customer, and never badger the customer in an attempt to win back the business. Don't bad-mouth the competitor you lost out to just to make yourself look better, and don't blame your own company for not being able to meet the customer's needs. It is better to take a positive stance: I have a superior product, but I also have great competitors. A customer once said, "My pet peeve is when sales reps don't sell their own company or defend it in front of the customer, but defend themselves and blame their company."

Above all, don't take the decision personally. Though customers prefer to work with salespeople they get along with, in most cases their choice of supplier is based almost purely on business considerations; for example, the cost and quality of the product or service they buy or the terms and conditions of the sale.

Taking lost sales personally only leads to feelings of rejection and disappointment, which can lower your self-esteem and diminish your motivation. Focus instead on what you have accomplished and on what you can gain from the experience that will help you in the future.

ASK WHY

Probe to find out why the customer decided to go with a competitor. Talk to your contact (and any other decision makers involved), and ask why you lost the business. Determine if there's anything more you could have done to win—or win back—the account.

Identify and categorize the primary reasons for the separation. Did it have to do with:

- *Price?* How does your selling price compare to that of the competitor who won the account? Could you have offered a discount or adjusted your standard payment terms to make the sale?

- *Product?* Does your product or service live up to the customer's quality expectations? Could you have customized your product to better meet the customer's needs?

- *Terms and conditions?* Did the customer object to any of the terms and conditions you offered? Would a modified delivery schedule, for example, have made a difference to the customer?

- *You?* Did you do anything to offend or anger the customer? Was there anything about your behavior, selling approach, or interpersonal style that worked against you? Sometimes a salesperson can create a wholly negative reaction; a customer relates that "a young rep bulldozed his way in, was rude to the receptionist, was arrogant in the call, then rang back and was very pushy and nearly lost his temper. That rep was banned from the business and all his efforts at contact were refused."

Be an optimist. Consider the lost sale a learning opportunity for both you and your organization, and determine what you should do differently to improve your sales results with other customers.

MAINTAIN THE RELATIONSHIP

Just because a customer decides to go with a competitor doesn't mean that he or she thinks poorly of you. Therefore, if it's appropriate, look for opportunities to get new business from the customer: Ask for referrals inside and outside the customer's company, and determine if there's a possibility that you might work together in the future. To increase the chances of that happening, maintain a good relationship with a customer that you've lost. Make sure your knowledge of his or her business and industry remains up-to-date and continue to demonstrate your value as a business resource.

Most important, check in periodically with lost customers to determine how well they're doing and how satisfied they are with the suppliers they chose. Keep them informed of any changes in your product, service, or organization that might make a difference in how they think of you and lead them to reconsider you as a supplier. Follow the advice of one salesperson who says to be confident that your product is better and that you can introduce something that's better for the customer in the long term.

> You should have positive thoughts, not only about your job, but about the world.

More Tips

■ *Don't exert undue influence.* Never try to influence a customer's decision by offering gifts to "sweeten" the sale (e.g., tickets to a sports event or hard-to-get theater tickets). This tactic can get you into trouble. Most customers today would consider it bribery—and highly unprofessional—while those that are willing to accept your offer might expect similar inducements in the future. To avoid either dilemma, focus on winning the sale through the merits of your product or service and the business value you can bring to the customer.

> Look at your work as a career, not just a job. Top salespeople have high integrity, they're ethical and professional, and they have drive, mental energy, and an "I want to win" attitude.

■ *Maintain a realistic outlook.* Successful salespeople maintain a balance between optimism and realism. They know that they have to remain upbeat—to create a positive impression on their customers and position their product or service in a favorable light. But they also know that they face stiff competition these days and that they can't expect to make every sale. They adopt a winning attitude, but they're also able to maintain their confidence and composure when they lose a sale.

19 LESSON

LEVERAGE YOUR PERFORMANCE THROUGH COACHING

Alligator Trap
Relying on Input from Others Is Risky

Alligators don't trust others enough to ask for advice. In the swamp, everyone's a predator, but good salespeople welcome input from others. After all, you can have the right knowledge, skills, and attitude to succeed as well as efficient business processes and advanced technologies. But the very best people in any profession know that their success won't be sustained without good coaching.

This is especially true in sales. Fast-changing market dynamics—the economy, the competition, new products and services—and your own organization's objectives make it essential to provide coaching to all salespeople. Coaching helps reinforce your training, guide your performance, and ensure alignment between your selling practices and your organization's business strategy. Training is not a one-time event; it's an ongoing process that extends beyond the initial commitment in the classroom. Coaching is an integral part of this process. When people leave a training session, they may be at their peak, but this soon evaporates without coaching and reinforcement.

If you don't have a good coach, find one. It could be your sales manager, a sales executive, or a peer. No matter who your coach is, seek constructive feedback on your strengths and weaknesses and help in honing your skills. Find someone who will be committed to helping you achieve your goals and those of your organization.

SEEK FEEDBACK

From your coach, you receive the one-on-one feedback and encouragement you need to improve your relationship-building skills with customers and to achieve better sales results. By providing critical support and personal attention, your coach helps you adapt what you learn from your manager, from co-workers, and from training programs to your own unique selling challenges.

> **On a scale of 1 to 10, sales coaching ranks an 11. It is extremely important.**

Your coach can provide you with guidance and direction in:

- *Call preparation.* Work with your coach to identify prospects, evaluate their sales potential, and establish sales call objectives.

- *Account planning.* You can draw from your coach's expertise when you're working to develop sales strategies and prioritize sales activities.

- *Sales negotiations.* Ask your coach to participate when you're conducting a difficult sales negotiation and to evaluate your effectiveness.

- *Sales presentations.* Have your coach sit in on several presentations you deliver to customers and identify areas where you can improve your presentation skills.

> Coaching can increase a salesperson's knowledge and set up the conditions necessary for self-development. It increases the self-confidence of the salesperson and creates a dialogue about performance.

MEET REGULARLY

Coaching is essential for new salespeople, but it can also benefit those who are more experienced, especially salespeople who are new hires and those selling to new businesses or industries. For maximum effectiveness, coaching should be conducted on a regular basis.

There are several ways you can work together regularly with your coach to evaluate and improve your performance:

- *Joint calls.* Once a week or several times a month, your coach and you can participate jointly in a sales call. Follow this with a thorough debriefing session.
- *Refresher sessions.* Meet with your coach on a weekly or biweekly basis to review and practice critical selling skills that you've learned in a training program.
- *Skills modeling.* You can refine your selling skills by periodically going on sales calls with your coach to observe how he or she uses them or by role-playing with your coach.

Your coach acts as your mirror, reflecting back to you your ongoing progress in the training relationship. Here are a few sample coaching questions:

- Do your customers view you as a consultant?
- Do your customers view you as different from other salespeople they deal with?
- Do your customers view you as someone they want to see again?
- Do your customers view you as someone they receive value from?

Asking these questions allows you to refine and sharpen your technique and helps you to learn how to be a unique resource to your customers.

DEVELOP A PLAN

Coaching works best when it's structured and ongoing—a routine practice that you commit yourself to. Work with your coach to establish a developmental game plan, one that establishes specific objectives and outlines a timetable for improvement.

Make sure your plan covers all the skills and abilities that contribute to your sales performance: interpersonal and communication skills, problem-solving and planning skills, team skills, and negotiation skills as well as your knowledge of your product or service, your customers' businesses, and your competitors.

Finally, measure and document your progress. Keep a file of your coach's evaluations along with other materials relating to your performance (e.g., customer surveys, revenue reports), and use this information when setting new improvement targets.

If your company doesn't provide a developmental coach, find one. Don't try to accomplish your sales improvement program by yourself. Practice, practice, practice—animals, children, and customers can smell fear. You must practice beforehand or you will end up practicing on the customer and you won't be performing consultatively.

More Tips

- *Enlist multiple coaches.* Coaching relationships can be established in a variety of ways. Your sales manager may act as your coach, your organization may designate a coach for you, or you may be allowed to choose your own coach. If you have the freedom to select anyone you want, you might suggest two or three names. By enlisting multiple coaches, you can make progress in a number of areas by working with people who excel in each.

- *Identify training needs.* The personal, informal approach used in coaching is highly effective for providing individualized attention to your professional development. You also can benefit significantly from formal training programs, especially those that focus on specific skills that you've identified as critical areas for improvement. To achieve the best results from training, conduct a needs analysis with your coach and then review available sales training programs with a training specialist. A salesperson who wants to do something about improving his or her skills and is keen to progress—and whose coaching is designed to meet those needs—is bound to succeed.

SUMMARY

ARE YOU PREPARED TO JOURNEY THROUGH
THE WETLANDS?   Or will you end up as a pair of shoes?

Remember I told you I used to sell computers? Well, the head of the company—the guy that fired me years ago—now owns a shoe company. He said he knew what I was really made of and thinks I would be an asset in his shoe company. I told him I always knew I had a future in shoes. He said he agreed and I would look great in a size 9½ medium.

Within the sales arena, alligators are quickly becoming an endangered species. Whenever they surface in the business world these days, most customers know enough to seek cover or swim away in the opposite direction. Though there are still salespeople who apply the alligator's predatory techniques—to make a killing quickly, no matter what the long-term costs—achieving success in sales today requires a totally different approach.

Avoiding the alligator trap involves discipline, hard work, and a commitment to customers. There's no quick-hit strategy that salespeople can use to win over customers and retain their loyalty. Instead, salespeople must adopt a more thoughtful approach and develop solid capabilities in the four areas critical to selling today: building long-term relationships with customers, practicing effective selling skills, recognizing and managing buyer attitudes, and establishing mutually beneficial business partnerships.

So whenever you're tempted to resort to the tactics an alligator might use, remember that the heyday of this reptile has long since past. To meet the needs and high expectations of today's customers, selling has evolved into a profession that requires intelligence, skillfulness, and creativity.

Enjoy the journey and good selling!

INDEX

ABOUT THE AUTHORS

Edward R. Del Gaizo, Ph.D. is director of research services at Learning International, a worldwide leader in sales and service training. In this capacity, he consults with customers on a variety of research and measurement issues, and internally on product development and marketing. For more than a decade, he has extensively studied successful salespeople and sales organizations, with an emphasis on sustaining customer relationships and loyalty. He has given presentations at several national associations, written articles for a variety of training and personnel journals, and has authored chapters in books on sales training and career development. His first job was selling soda at New York's Shea Stadium, where he quickly learned that selling was more than shouting what you had to offer.

Kevin J. Corcoran is vice president of sales and marketing for the Sales Process Automation Division at Learning International. As a frequent consultant and lecturer on consultative selling and sales process, Corcoran's presentations have explored the practices of leading global companies as they strive for enhanced profitability and exceptional sales performance in an increasingly complex and competitive marketplace. During his 15-year tenure at Learning International, Corcoran has managed national accounts, developed and coached sales teams, implemented marketing strategies, and led the revision and launch of Learning International's flagship product, *Professional Selling Skills (PSS)*. His present responsibilities include the integration of sales process and technology with Learning International's new sales process automation software, HeatSeeker. He is a co-author of Learning International's first book, *High Performance Sales*

Organizations: Creating Competitive Advantage in the Global Marketplace.

David J. Erdman is president and chief executive officer of Learning International. He came to Learning International in 1994 from Kaset International, where he served as the customer service training company's president and chief executive officer since 1986. Both Learning International and Kaset are part of Times Mirror, a $3.6 billion media communications company. Before joining Kaset, Erdman was vice president of product development at Deltak, Inc., which develops self-study computer skills training products. He also spent several years in public broadcasting, most notably WTTW in Chicago. While at WTTW, Erdman was awarded an "Emmy" for television direction of musical programs and a Corporation for Public Broadcasting award for his work on documentaries.